Should we believe in God, Allah or other Deities?

By
Frank Hegyi

**Published by
Frank Hegyi Publications Ottawa, Ontario, Canada**
www.hegyipublication.com

**© Frank Hegyi – 2017
ISBN 978-0-9940201-4-7**
fshegyi1575@rogers.com

All rights reserved

Contents

Acknowledgement 7
Introduction 9
Christians Religion 13
The Review of Christianity 19
   The Roman Catholic Church 19
      The population 19
      The churches 20
   The Anglican Church 26
      The Population 26
      The Church 29
   The Presbyterian Church..................................... 34
      The Population 34
      The Church 36
   The United Church of Canada 42
      The Population 42
      The Church 44
   The Christian Reformed Churches 50
      The Population 50
      The Church 51
   Jehovah Witnesses 57

- The Mormon Church 63
- Islam 71
  - Summary of Muslim Religion 76
    - Population 76
    - Sufism 80
    - Shi'a, a branch is Islam 84
    - Sunni Islam 86
    - Ahmadiyya sect of Islam 89
- Judaism 93
  - The Jewish People 99
    - The Population 99
    - The Religion 101
- Hinduism 107
- Chinese Religion 121
  - Buddhism 122
  - Confucianism 124
  - Taoism 125
  - Islam 126
  - Christianity 127
  - Other beliefs 127
- The Buddhist Religion 133
  - Key facts 136

- The Dalai Lama 137
- Sikhism religion 145
  - Sikhism and abortion 147
  - Sikh moral thinking 148
  - DharamYudh - Just War 149
  - Sikhism and birth control 150
  - Sikhism and organ donation 150
- Spiritualist church 153
- Baha'i religion 159
- Jains Religion 165
- Shiniest Religion 171
- Tao Religion 175
- Zoroastrianism Religion 183
- Non Religions 191
  - Atheist. 193
  - Anti-theist. 194
  - Agnostic. 195
  - Skeptic. 196
  - Freethinker. 196
  - Humanist. 197
  - Pantheist. 198
- Is it God, Allah or other Deities watching over us?. 201

Acknowledgement

I have always been fascinated by religion. I was growing up in the Roman Catholic Church in Hungary. I had a protected education about religion; I was taught that the Roman Catholic Church was the only true religion, and protestant was second, and Jews were third.

When I left Hungary at age 18, I opened my eyes about religion. Besides the Roman Catholic Church, I became familiar with the Presbyterian Church, the Anglican Church, The United Church and the Jewish rites. I am now a realistic believer in religion.

Later on in my senior years I became active again in the church; I am on the Roman Catholic Church Council and I attend mass regularly (I am a greeter for the church membership). I believe that a God exists, but also I respect that some other people have deities that are called different.

Religion is the vehicle that people have in getting together in a congregation to worship and practice good living.

This book is about religion and highlighting the different worships that people are engaging. The aim of the book is to present an unbiased view that all religious beliefs are leading the way to a Supreme Being they call it God, Allah or other deities.

Introduction

The worldwide percentage of adherence by Religion in 2005 is shown below[1]. Christians are the largest number, then Muslims, Hindus, Non-religion, Chinese Universe, Buddhist and so on.

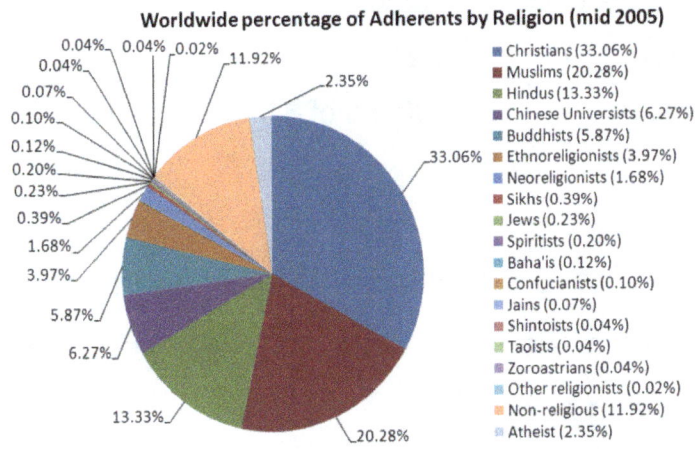

This number changes slightly in 2010 when the population is divided us as follows:

---

[1] https://www.cs.mcgill.ca/~rwest/link-suggestion/wpcd_2008-09_augmented/images/785/78568.png.htm

Christians	31.5%
Muslims	23.2%
Unaffiliated	16.3%
Hindu	15.5%
Buddhist	7.1%
Folk Religion	5.9%
Other Religion	0.8%
Jewish	0.2%
Total:	100.0% of 6,895,890,000 total[2]

The Christians are broken up in various groups or denominations as presented by the following tree.

---

[2] http://www.pewforum.org/files/2014/01/global-religion-full.pdf

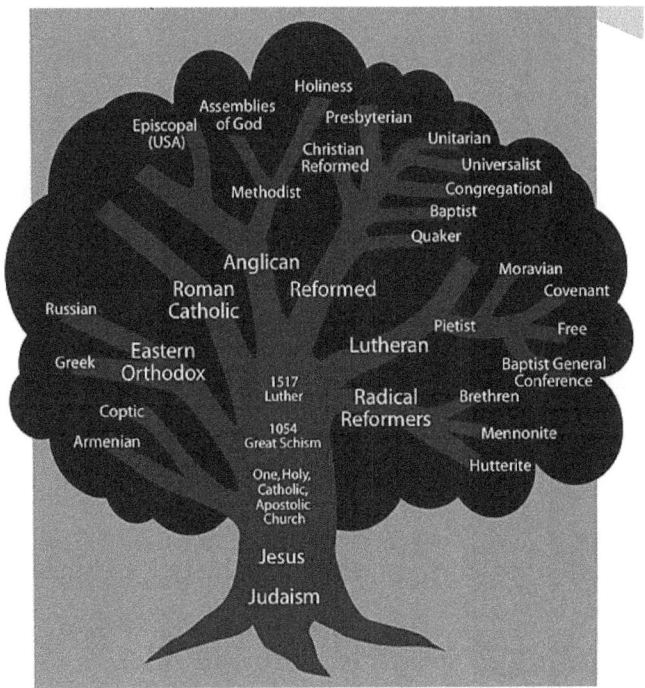

Believing in God and Deity is one of the highest importance in humans. On the Internet, there is a good documentation of religious practices; some of these appear in this publication (with references to authors).

Christians Religion

The Christian religion[3] is the largest number (33.06%) and the Roman Catholic religion is the largest among them.

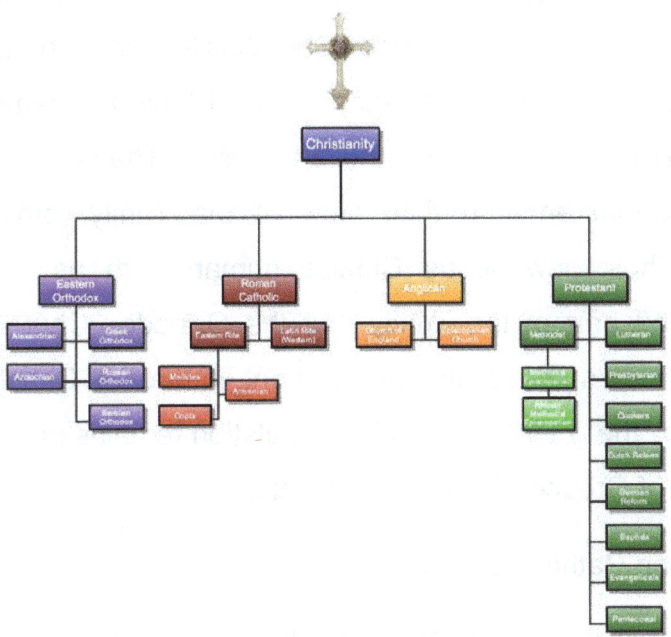

---

[3]http://macaulay.cuny.edu/eportfolios/drabik10website/tools/religion-flow-chart/

Eastern Orthodox

The Eastern Orthodox Church has always reflected a more philosophical branch of Christianity. Part of their beliefs is that religion is a personal experience. There is often no exact definition of religious truth. The Orthodox Church is led by the head bishops (although these bishops don't have the same power as the Pope does in Catholicism). They have a slight difference in their view of the Trinity; other branches view Jesus Christ's human form as the second part of the Trinity, but the Orthodox Church believe it's the divine pre-existent nature of Christ. Today the greatest Orthodox population remains in the area of Greece, Turkey and Russia.

Roman Catholic Church

The Roman Catholic Church is, the biggest denomination of Christianity with more than one billion followers. Catholicism is dominant in Western nations like Italy, Spain, Latin America, and even the United States. The Roman Catholic beliefs include the special authority of the pope, the ability of saints to intercede on behalf of believers, the concept of Purgatory as a place of afterlife purification before entering Heaven.

Anglican

The roots of the Anglican Church lie within its first church, the Church of England. Just like Protestantism, Anglicanism was formed in an attempt to reform the Roman Catholic Church (Anglicanism formed just 20 years after Protestantism). In Anglicanism, there is no central source of power: no Pope (just a lead bishop) and no Patriarch. A unique aspect of Anglicanism is the Book of Common Prayer. This prayer book forms the historical basis for most Anglican liturgy.

The Anglican Church was originally spread through English colonization, but this also led to the several independent Anglican Churches. The most notable of the Anglican Churches are the Church of England and the Episcopalian Church. The Episcopalian Church has many similarities to the

Church of England, but one vital difference is the lack of monarchial ties in the Episcopalian Church. This process was repeated through English colonies; although the Church of England was the first branch of Anglicanism, today there are over 40 independent national Anglican Churches.

Protestant

The Protestant church goes directly to the Word of God for instruction, and to the throne of grace in his devotions. Protestantism was formed on three fundamental principles: scripture, justification by faith, and universal priesthood of believers. The Scripture states that the Bible is the only source of authority for the church and that the priest's word are insignificant but not absolute. Justification by faith alone allows salvation only through faith, this was an attempt to reform the Church's accepting of donations. The universal priesthood of believers encourages followers to read the Bible and take action in all church related activities. Today, the Protestant Church has grown too many different denominations such as Lutheran, Methodist, Baptist, and Presbyterian and so on.

The Review of Christianity

The Roman Catholic Church

The population

According to the CIA Fact book[4] the five countries with the largest number of Catholics are, in decreasing order of population, Brazil (125,000,000), Mexico (98,820,000), the Philippines (81,400,000), the United States (66,560,000), and Italy (50,474,000). Canada is 13,843,000. According to the Census of the 2016 Pontifical Yearbook, the number of Catholics in the world was about 1.272 billion at the end of 2014.

Between 2005 and 2014, the world's Catholic population rose from 1.115 billion (17.3% of the world's population) to 1.272 billion (17.8%), according to statistics made public by the Holy See Press. During that time period, the Catholic population soared by 41% in Africa and 20% in Asia, approximately double the

---

[4] CIA Factbook 2015

rate of population growth on each continent (23.8% in Africa, 9.6% in Asia). During the same time period, the Catholic population increased by 11.7% in North and South America, 2% in Europe, and 15.9% in Oceania.

The churches

In monotheism, God[5] is conceived of as the Supreme Being and the principal object of faith. The concept of God as described by most theologians includes the attributes of omniscience (infinite knowledge), omnipotence (unlimited power), omnipresence (present everywhere), divine simplicity, and as having an eternal and necessary existence. Many theologians also describe God as being omnibenevolent (perfectly good) and all loving. God is most often held to be incorporeal (immaterial) and to be without gender, yet the concept of God actively creating the universe (as opposed to passively) has caused many religions to describe God using masculine

---

[5] God, Wikipedia

terminology, using such terms as "Him" or "Father". Furthermore, some religions (such as Judaism) attribute only a purely grammatical "gender" to God. God are related to conceptions of transcendence (being outside nature) and immanence (being in nature, in the world) of God, with positions of synthesis such as the "immanent transcendence" of Chinese theology.

God has been conceived as either personal or impersonal. In theism, God is the creator and sustainer of the universe, while in deism, God is the creator, but not the sustainer, of the universe. God is the universe itself. In atheism, God is not believed to exist, while God is deemed unknown or unknowable within the context of agnosticism. God has also been conceived as the source of all moral obligation, and the "greatest conceivable existent". Many notable philosophers have developed arguments for and against the existence of God; but they are just arguments.

In 2014, nearly half (48%) of the world's Catholics lived in North and South America. 22.6% lived in Europe, 17% in Africa, 10.9% in Asia, and 0.8% in

Oceania. Between 2005 and 2014, the number of priests increased from 406,411 to 415,792, while the number of permanent deacons rose from 33,000 to 44,566. The number of priests rose significantly in Africa (by 32.6%) and Asia (by 27.1%), which declining in Europe (by 8%). About 97.5% of permanent deacons live in North America, South America, or Europe.

Despite substantial gains in Africa and Asia, the number of religious brothers worldwide decreased from 54,708 in 2005 to 54,559 in 2014, while the number of religious sisters fell by 10.8% to 682,729.

The worldwide surge in the number of seminarians rose from 63,882 (1978) to 120,616 (2011), and then fell to 116,939 (2014). Between 2005 and 2014, the number of seminarians soared in Africa (by 30.9%) and in Asia (by 29.4%) but plummeted in Europe (by 21.7%) and declined in North and South America (by 1.9%)[6].

---

[6]World's Catholic population approaches 1.3 billion 2016.

A Palm Sunday celebration in a Catholic church before Vatican II.[7]

A wedding day in the Roman Catholic Church[8] after Vatican II.

---

[7]https://en.wikipedia.org/wiki/Catholic_Church
[8]http://www.traditionalcatholicpriest.com/wp-content/uploads/2014/09/Katies-wedding-II.jpg

The costumes worn by religious nuns; it is rapidly disappearing.

St Peters Basilica in Rome[9]

---

[9]https://en.wikipedia.org/wiki/Mass_in_the_Catholic_Church#/media/File:StPetersBasilicaEarlyMorning.jpg

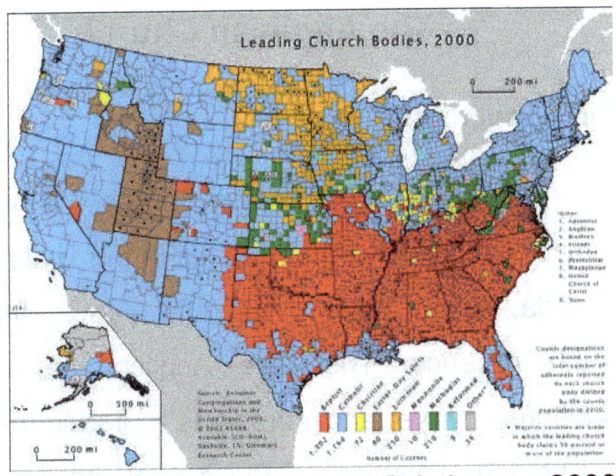

Leading church bodies in U.S.A. in year 2000.

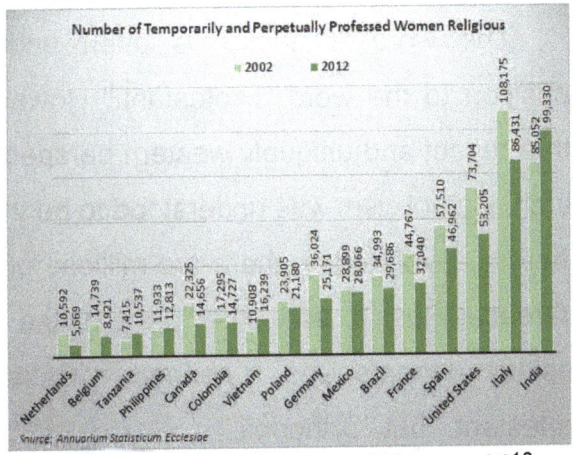

Religious sisters around the world[10]

---

[10]https://www.google.com/search?q=sisters+of+religion

The Anglican Church

The Population

The Anglican Catholic Church[11] is worldwide body of Christians with churches in the United States, Canada, Great Britain, Australia, Africa, India, and South America. They are Anglican because our tradition of prayer and worship is rooted in the Church of England. They are Catholic because they believe and practice the universal or catholic faith of the church.

The word "Catholic" is often understood in opposition to the word "Protestant." However, this is both a recent and uniquely western perspective. In the church, Catholicism was understood to be the opposite of heresy. Even today, there are millions of Christians in Greece, Russia, and other parts of the world who consider themselves neither "Catholic" nor "Protestant," but "Orthodox."

---

[11]http://www.anglicancatholic.org/about-the-church

During the sixteenth century, the Church of England sought to modify certain beliefs and practices that had developed over the centuries and appeared unwise, or divergent from apostolic faith and practice. In doing so, the church did not abandon its Catholicism; rather it engaged in a process of reform. As Bishop John Bramhall wrote in the seventeenth century, "our religion is the same it was, our Church the same it was...differing only from what they were formerly, as a garden weeded from a garden un-weeded."

Anglicanism, is best understood as a reformed catholic faith. Likewise, they believe that the church is in need of continual renewal and reformation. It must oppose the errors of every age in order to "contend earnestly for the faith which was once delivered to the saints".

Henry VIII created the Anglican church in anger over the Pope's refusal to grant his divorce, but the historical record indicates that Henry spent most of his reign challenging the authority of Rome, and that the divorce issue was just one of a series of acts that collectively split the English church from the Roman church in much the same way that the Orthodox church had split off five hundred years before.

With a membership estimated at around 85 million members, the Anglican Communion is the third largest Christian communion in the world, after the Catholic Church and the Eastern Orthodox Church. Some of these churches are known as Anglican, such as the Anglican Church of Canada, due to their historical link to England (*Ecclesia Anglicana* means "English Church"). Some other associated churches have a separate name. Each independent church has its own doctrine and liturgy, aligned in most cases on that of the Church of England; and each church has its own legislative process and overall episcopal polity, under the leadership of a local primate.

The Church

Anglicanism[12], in its structures, theology and forms of worship, is commonly understood as a distinct Christian tradition representing a middle ground between what are perceived to be the extremes of the claims of 16th-century Roman Catholicism and Protestantism of that era. As such, it is often referred to as being a "middle way" between these traditions.

The faith of Anglicans is founded in the Scriptures and the Gospels, the traditions of the Apostolic Church, the historical episcopate, the first seven ecumenical councils and the early Church Fathers and among these Fathers, especially those active during the five initial centuries of Christianity. Anglicans understand the Old and New Testaments as "containing all things necessary for salvation" and as being the rule and ultimate standard of faith. 'Reason' and 'Tradition' are seen as valuable means to interpret Scripture, but there is no full mutual agreement among

---

[12]https://en.wikipedia.org/wiki/Anglicanism

Anglicans *exactly how* Scripture, Reason and Tradition interact with each other. Anglicans understand the Apostles' Creed as the baptismal symbol and the Nicene Creed as the sufficient statement of the Christian faith.

Anglicans believe the catholic and apostolic faith is revealed in Holy Scripture and the Catholic creeds and interpret these in light of the Christian tradition of the historic church, scholarship, reason and experience.

Anglicans celebrate the traditional sacraments, with special emphasis being given to the Eucharist, the Lord's Supper or the Mass. The Eucharist is central to worship for most Anglicans as a communal offering of prayer and praise in which the life, death and resurrection of Jesus Christ are proclaimed through prayer, reading of the Bible, singing, giving God thanks over the bread and wine for the innumerable benefits obtained through the passion of Christ. The breaking of the bread, and reception of the bread and wine as representing the body and blood of Christ as instituted at the Last Supper. Tradition, a considerable degree of liturgical freedom is permitted, and worship styles range from the simple to elaborate.

Unique to Anglicanism is the *Book of Common Prayer* (BCP), the collection of services that worshippers in most Anglican churches used for centuries. It was called *common prayer* originally because it was intended for use in all Church of England churches which had previously followed differing local liturgies. The term was kept when the church became international because all Anglicans used to share in its use around the world. Anglican churches in different countries have developed other service books, the Prayer Book is still acknowledged as one of the ties that bind Anglicans together.

The Anglican Centre has been at the heart of dialogue between Anglicans and Roman Catholics since 1966.

The Archbishop of Canterbury (left) hosted a reception at Lambeth Palace in the presence of The Prince of Wales.

From left: Bishop of Derby, Archbishop of Canterbury and Anglican Alliance Co-Executive Director at the Forum on Modern Slavery held in Istanbul

The Presbyterian Church

The Population

The vision of the Presbyterian Church or its original form the Church of Scotland is to be a church which seeks to inspire the people of Scotland with the Good News of Jesus Christ through enthusiastic worshipping, witnessing, nurturing and serving communities.

The Church of Scotland[13] is one of the largest organisations in the country in Scotland. They have over 350,000 members, with more regularly involved in local congregations and our work. Within the organisation, we have around 800 ministers serving in parishes and chaplaincies, supported by more than 1500 professional and administrative staff. Most of our parishes are in Scotland, but there are also churches in England, Europe and overseas.

---

[13] http://www.churchofscotland.org.uk/about_us

The Church of Scotland works with communities worldwide. These aims are that has a pivotal role in Scottish society and indeed religion throughout the world.

The responsibility for holding and preserving most Church properties rests with the General Trustees. They also authorise sales and property, get alterations at buildings, assist local congregations with maintenance and improvement work and give financial assistance in a number of ways. The trustees can also provide advice and financial assistance to local congregations to help with maintaining and improving their buildings. The Church's Central Properties Department has responsibility for redevelopment of Church property and managing existing property.

The General Assembly has the authority to make laws determining how The Church of Scotland operates. It is also the highest court of the Church in which cases can be heard in matters of litigation. The other courts in the Church are the kirk session and the presbytery. The Assembly comprises around 850 commissioners who are ministers, elders and members of the diaconate. It meets at the same time in May each year for a week, usually in the Assembly Hall on the Mound in central Edinburgh. The first General Assembly was held in December 1560, which was the year of the Scottish Reformation and which marks the beginning of the Church of Scotland. The General Assembly acts as the highest court of the Church of Scotland, and has the authority to make laws determining how the Church of Scotland operates. A full list of these laws, referred to as acts and regulations, dating back to 1929, is available to download on the website[14].

The Church

While the Church of Scotland traces its roots back to the earliest Christians in Scotland[15], its identity was principally shaped by the Scottish Reformation of 1560. At that point, many in the then church in Scotland

---

[14] https://en.wikipedia.org/wiki/Presbyterian_polity
[15] https://en.wikipedia.org/wiki/Church_of_Scotland

broke with Rome, in a process of Protestant reform led, among others, by John Knox. It reformed its doctrines and government, drawing on the principles of John Calvin which Knox had been exposed to while living in Geneva, Switzerland. In 1560, an assembly of some nobles, lairds and burgesses, as well as several churchmen, claiming in defiance of the Queen to be a Scottish Parliament, abolished papal jurisdiction and approved the *Scots Confession*. However, it did not accept many of the principles laid out in Knox's *First Book of Discipline*, which argued that all of the assets of the old church should pass to the new. The 1560 Reformation Settlement was not ratified by the crown, as the monarch, Mary, Queen of Scots, a Catholic, refused to do so, and the question of church government also remained unresolved. In 1572 the acts of 1560 were finally approved by the young King James VI, the son of Queen Mary, but the Concordat of Leith also allowed the crown to appoint bishops with the church's approval. John Knox himself had no clear views on the office of bishop. They renamed as 'superintendents', but in response to the new Concordat a Presbyterian party emerged headed by Andrew Melville, the author of the *Second Book of Discipline*.

Melville and his supporters enjoyed some temporary successes—most notably in the Golden Act of 1592, which gave parliamentary approval to Presbyterian courts. James VI, who succeeded to the English throne in 1603 as James I, believed that Presbyterianism was incompatible with monarchy, declaring "No bishop, no king" and by skillful manipulation of both church and state, steadily reintroduced parliamentary and then diocesan episcopacy. By the time he died in 1625, the Church of Scotland had a full panel of bishops and archbishops. General Assemblies met only at times and places approved by the Crown.

The Church of Scotland Offices are located at 121 George Street, Edinburgh. These imposing buildings were designed in a Scandinavian-influenced style by the architect Sydney Mitchell and built in 1909–

1911 for the United Free Church of Scotland. Following the union of the churches in 1929 a matching extension was built in the 1930s.

The offices of the Moderator, Principal Clerk, General Treasurer, Law Department and all the Church councils are located at 121 George Street, with the exception of the Social Care Council. The Principal Clerk to the General Assembly is the Very Rev. John Chalmers. Each Council has its own Council Secretary who sit as a senior management team led by the Secretary to the Council of Assembly, currently the Rev Dr Martin Scott.

Since 1968, all ministries and offices in the church have been open to women and men on an equal basis. In 2004, Alison Elliot was chosen to be Moderator of the General Assembly, the first woman in the post and the first non-minister to be chosen since George Buchanan, four centuries before. In May 2007 the Rev Sheilagh M. Kesting became the first female minister to be Moderator. There are currently 218 serving female ministers, with 677 male ministers.

The Ordination of Elders in a Scottish Kirk

The first Scots Presbyterian church

Presbyterian worship today.

The United Church of Canada

The Population

The United Church of Canada is a mainline Reformed denomination and the largest Protestant Christian denomination in Canada. The United Church was founded in 1925 as a merger of four Protestant denominations with a total combined membership of about 600,000 members: the Methodist Church, Canada, the Congregational Union of Ontario and Quebec, two-thirds of the congregations of the Presbyterian Church in Canada, and the Association of Local Union Churches, a predominantly prairie-based movement. The Canadian Conference of the Evangelical United Brethren Church joined the United Church of Canada on 1 January 1968.

Membership peaked in 1964 at 1.1 million and has declined since that time. From 1991 to 2001, the number of people claiming an affiliation with the United Church decreased by 8%, the third largest decrease in mainstream Christian denominations in Canada.

Church statistics for the beginning of 2014 showed 450,886 members and approximately 2 million adherents. About 139,000 people attend services in 2,172 pastoral charges representing 3,016 congregations on a regular basis. According to the statistics released in May 2013 the United Church in Canada had 2,008,000 adherents, about 5.7% of the total Canadian population.

The United Church has a "council-based" structure, where each council (congregational, regional or denominational) have specific responsibilities. In some areas, each of these councils have sole authority, while in others, approval of other councils is required before action is taken. The policies of the church are inclusive and liberal: there are no restrictions of gender, sexual orientation or marital status for a person considering entering the ministry; interfaith marriages are recognized; communion is offered to all Christian adults and children, regardless of denomination or age.

The Church

The voice and face of the church is the Moderator[16], who is elected to a three-year term at each General Council. The duties of the Moderator include:

- Giving leadership to the church, "quickening in the hearts of the people a sense of God as revealed in Christ, and heartening and strengthening the whole United Church";
- Visiting pastoral charges across the country, "giving sympathetic guidance and counsel in all its affairs";
- Being the primary spokesperson for the United Church; and
- Presiding at the meetings of the General Council, Executive, and its Sub-Executive.

---

[16]https://en.wikipedia.org/wiki/United_Church_of_Canada#Interfaith_relations

Currently, Jordan Cantwell, an ordained minister from Saskatchewan, holds the position after her election August 13, 2015 at the 42nd General Council.

For the first 90 years of its existence, administration in the United Church was divided into four levels of governance, or "courts":

Pastoral charge (congregation)

The basic unit of the United Church is the pastoral charge, consisting of one or more congregations under the spiritual leadership of a minister or ministry team. A pastoral charge that has two or more congregations is described as a "two-point charge", "three-point charge", etc.

The pastoral charge is responsible for their day-to-day operations, including raising all of the money needed for staff, building maintenance and operation, worship, committee work and projects. This is generally done by taking up a collection from the congregation, but fundraising from the wider community is also allowed, as long as it does not involve games of chance such as raffles, lotteries, or bingo. The pastoral charge is also responsible for searching out and hiring church staff, including ministers, musicians and lay staff; maintenance and upkeep of their property and buildings; Christian development and education within the congregation (Sunday School, youth and adult confirmation classes, Bible study, etc.); outreach projects to the community and wider world; and other day-to-day functions.

Policy decisions at this level are usually made by a congregational Board or Council, which can take one of the several forms listed in *The Manual*. However, budgets and finances, election of Board members and changes to ministry-pastoral relations must be approved at a meeting of the full congregation.

Presbytery

There are 85 presbyteries within the United Church, each being a collection of about 20–60 pastoral charges. All members of the Order of Ministry, active and retired, Recognized Designated Lay Ministers under appointment as well as several other classifications of lay members are members of the presbytery—"presbyters"—rather than members of their pastoral charge. Each pastoral charge may also send delegates from the congregation to assist in decision-making. The presbytery is responsible for care and oversight of the pastoral charges within it. When a pastoral charge is seeking a new minister, the presbytery provides presbyters who help to assess the congregation's ministerial needs as well as taking part in the search process.

Conference

Presbyteries are gathered up into one of 13 conferences. The conference is responsible for the training and education of candidates for ministry, for overall church mission strategy, and for electing commissioners to attend general councils.

General Council

This is the church's highest legislative court. Every three years, ministers and lay commissioners who have been elected by the Conferences meet to set church policy and choose a new Moderator. An Executive and Sub-Executive govern between meetings of the council.

The Moderator of the United Church in Canada,
The right Reverend Jordan Cantwell

The Knox United Church in MB

The Christian Reformed Churches

The Population

The Christian Reformed Church (CRC)[17] includes just over one thousand congregations across the United States and Canada. About 75 percent of the churches are in the United States and 25 percent are in Canada. We're one of only a few binational denominations: rather than split into different churches at the 49th parallel, we're united.

Almost 300,000 people belong to the CRCNA—not a large number when you consider the population of our two countries. But they can accomplish a lot when we work together. The Christian Reformed Church is a diverse family of healthy congregations, assemblies, and ministries expressing the good news of God's kingdom that transforms lives and communities worldwide.

---

[17] https://www.crcna.org/welcome/beliefs

Our Mission
- We gather to praise God, listen to him, and respond.
- We nurture each other in faith and obedience to Christ.
- We love and care for one another as God's people.
- We commit ourselves to serve and to tell others about Jesus.
- We pursue God's justice and peace in every area of life.
- Our Calling

Closed captions are available in English, Korean and Spanish.

The Church

The bulk of what we believe we hold in common with the Christian church around the world and throughout the ages. Three creeds[18] adopted by the worldwide church centuries ago summarize the most important tenets of our faith: the Apostles' Creed, the Nicene Creed, and the Athanasian Creed.

To summarize these common beliefs, we'll use the text of the Apostles' Creed. But first an explanation. Despite its title, the Apostles' Creed was not written by the apostles or disciples who walked and talked with Jesus in the first century. Instead it is a compilation of what believers in the first centuries knew from written and oral testimony, which was then distilled into the essentials of the Christian faith. This creed was reworked by successive councils of the early Church. It was adopted in its present form before the end of the fourth century.

A quick look at the structure of the Apostles' Creed reveals one of the bedrock truths of the Christian faith: the Trinity. The creed is divided into three parts: God the Father, God the Son, and God the Holy Spirit.

---

[18]https://www.crcna.org/welcome/beliefs/basics-christianity

All Christians believe that the Bible reveals one God in three "persons." In other words, God is a perfect community of love.

God: I believe in God. The creed begins with a simple affirmation of belief in God. The following three sections describe the three persons of this one God.

God the Father: the Father almighty, creator of heaven and earth. The first person of the Trinity is the one Jesus revealed to us as "the Father." God is not some remote, unknowable spiritual entity. Rather God is our loving, powerful heavenly Father. We profess that God created heaven and earth and all that is in them. This profession affirms the goodness of creation and endows it with meaning and purpose. Further, all that is good and beautiful points to a Creator God. Thus all humans can know something about God through what creation reveals.

God the Son: I believe in Jesus Christ, his only Son, our Lord, who was conceived by the Holy Spirit and born of the Virgin Mary. He suffered under Pontius Pilate, was crucified, died, and was buried; he descended to hell. The third day he rose again from the dead. He ascended to heaven and is seated at the right hand of God the Father almighty. From there he will come to judge the living and the dead. We affirm that Jesus of Nazareth, though born of a woman, was more than a human being; he was actually God's Son and thus also God himself. As the Christ, Jesus fulfilled all the Old Testament prophecies about a Messiah who would redeem God's people. The life, death, and resurrection of Jesus are grounded in historical fact. After his earthly work of redemption was finished, Jesus took his place in heaven as Lord of all things. He will come again to make all things new.

God the Holy Spirit: I believe in the Holy Spirit, the holy Catholic Church, the communion of saints, the forgiveness of sins, the resurrection of the body, and the life everlasting. Amen. When Jesus ascended bodily to heaven, he promised his disciples a comforter, a source of power; one that would "lead them into all truth." This gift was the Holy Spirit. Ever since then, the Holy Spirit has dwelled in and empowered God's people. The Holy Spirit is the presence and power of God with us here and now, leading the church, uniting God's people, applying God's forgiveness to our broken lives, speaking to us, and spurring us individually and communally to godly living.

Calvin Christian Reformed Church

Craig Hoekema – Lead Pastor

Jehovah Witnesses

Jehovah's Witnesses[19] base their beliefs only on the text of the Bible and ignore "mere human speculations or religious creeds." They believe that the Bible is the Word of God and consider its 66 books to be divinely inspired and historically accurate.

Members reject the sinful values of the secular world and maintain a degree of separation from non-believers - they are "in the world" but not "of the world". Witnesses do not celebrate Christmas or Easter because they believe that these festivals are based on (or massively contaminated by) pagan customs and religions. They point out that Jesus did not ask his followers to mark his birthday.

Jehovah's Witnesses maintain a degree of separation from the world. They claim that they are in but not of the world. Unlike the members of more extreme separatist movements, Witnesses both live

---

[19] http://www.bbc.co.uk/religion/religions/witnesses/ataglance/glance.shtml

and work among the secular community and send their children to secular schools. Witnesses discourage participation in university education for its own sake.

They also refuse military service, voting in elections, and taking part in most religious festivals and secular celebrations like birthdays. In countries with compulsory national service most Witnesses will accept civilian service as an alternative to military service. Certain civic obligations, such as jury service, are seen as a matter for individual decision according to the dictates of conscience.

The church is strongly millennial and believes that humanity is now in the 'last days' and that the final battle between good and evil will happen soon.

In 1870, Charles Taze Russell[20] and others formed a group in Pittsburgh, Pennsylvania to study the Bible. During the course of his ministry, Russell disputed many beliefs of mainstream Christianity including immortality of the soul, hellfire, predestination,

---

[20]https://en.wikipedia.org/wiki/Jehovah's_Witnesses

the fleshly return of Jesus Christ, the Trinity, and the burning up of the world. From 1879, *Watch Tower* supporters gathered as autonomous congregations to study the Bible topically. Thirty congregations were founded, and during 1879 and 1880, Russell visited each to provide the format he recommended for conducting meetings. As congregations continued to form during Russell's ministry, they each remained self-administrative, functioning under the Congregationalist style of church governance.

Jehovah's Witnesses believe death is a state of non-existence with no consciousness. There is no Hell of fiery torment; Hades and Sheol are understood to refer to the condition of death, termed the common grave. Jehovah's Witnesses consider the soul to be a life or a living body that can die. Jehovah's Witnesses believe that humanity is in a sinful state, from which release is only possible by means of Jesus' shed blood as a ransom, or atonement, for the sins of humankind.

As of August 2016, Jehovah's Witnesses report an average of 8.13 million *publishers*—the term they use for members actively involved in preaching—in 119,485 congregations. In 2016, these reports indicated over 1.98 billion hours spent in preaching and "Bible study" activity. Since the mid-1990s, the number of peak publishers has increased from 4.5 million to 8.34 million. In the same year, they conducted Bible studies with over 10.1 million individuals, including those conducted by Witness parents with their children. Jehovah's Witnesses estimate their current worldwide growth rate to be 1.8% per year.

International headquarters in Warwick, New York

Worship at Kingdom hall

The Mormon Church

The Mormon[21] Church is a Christian restorationist church that is considered by its followers to be the restoration of the original church founded by Jesus Christ. The church is headquartered in Salt Lake City, Utah, and has established congregations and built temples worldwide. According to the church, it has over 74,000 missionaries and a membership of over 15 million. It is ranked by the National Council of Churches as the fourth-largest Christian denomination in the United States. It is the largest denomination in the Latter Day Saint movement founded by Joseph Smith during the period of religious revival known as the Second Great Awakening.

During the 20th century, the church grew substantially and became an international organization, due in part to the spread of missionaries around the globe. In 2000, the church reported 60,784

---

[21] https://en.wikipedia.org/wiki/The_Church_of_Jesus_Christ_of_Latter-day_Saints

missionaries and global church membership stood at just over 11 million. Worldwide membership surpassed 13 million in 2007 and reached 14 million in July 2010, with about six million of those within the United States. However, it is estimated based on demographic studies from the early 1990s that only one-third of the total worldwide membership (about 4 million people as of 2005) are considered "active churchgoers." The church cautions against overemphasis of growth statistics for comparison with other churches because relevant factors—including activity rates and death rates, methodology used in registering or counting members, what factors constitute membership, and geographical variations—are rarely accounted for in the comparisons.

The theology of the LDS Church consists of a combination of biblical doctrines with modern revelations and other commentary by LDS leaders, particularly Joseph Smith. The most authoritative sources of theology are the faith's canon of four religious texts, called the "standard works". Included in the standard works are the Bible, the Book of Mormon, the Doctrine and Covenants, and the Pearl of Great Price. The Book of Mormon is said by the church to be "Another Testament of Jesus Christ" that Smith translated from buried golden plates. The LDS Church believes that the Angel Moroni told Smith about these golden plates and guided him to find them buried in the Hill Cumorah. The church believes that this Angel Moroni is at least partial fulfilment of Revelation 14:6 in the Bible. The church characterizes the Book of Mormon as "the most correct of any book on earth and the keystone of [the] religion".

The Bible, also part of the church's canon, is believed to be "the word of God as far as it is translated correctly." Most often, the church uses the Authorized King James Version. Sometimes, however, parts of the Joseph Smith Translation of the Bible (corrections and restorations of assertedly damaged or lost passages) are considered authoritative. Some excerpts of Smith's translation have been included in the Pearl of Great Price, which also includes further translations by Smith and church historical items. Other historical items and revelations are found in the Doctrine and Covenants

The LDS Church is organized in a hierarchical priesthood structure administered by men. Latter-day Saints believe that Jesus leads the church through revelation and has chosen a single man, called "the Prophet" or President of the Church, as his spokesman on the earth. The current president is Thomas S. Monson. While there have been exceptions in the past, he and two counselors are normally ordained apostles and form the First Presidency, the presiding body of the church; twelve other apostles form the Quorum of the Twelve Apostles. When a president dies, his successor is invariably the most senior member of the Quorum of the Twelve (the one who has been an apostle the longest), who reconstitutes a new First Presidency. These men, and the other male members of the church-wide leadership (including the first two Quorums of Seventy and the Presiding Bishopric) are called general authorities. They exercise both ecclesiastical and administrative leadership over the church and direct the efforts of regional leaders down to the local level. General authorities and mission presidents work full-time and typically receive stipends from church funds or investments.

Under the leadership of the priesthood hierarchy are five auxiliary organizations that fill various roles in the church: Relief Society (a women's organization), the Young Men and Young Women organizations (for adolescents ages 12 to 18), Primary (an organization for children up to age 12), and Sunday School (which provides a variety of Sunday classes for adolescents and adults). Women serve as presidents and counselors in the presidencies of the Relief Society, Young Women, and Primary, while men serve as presidents and counselors of the Young Men and Sunday school. The church also operates several programs and organizations in the fields of proselytizing, education, and church welfare such as LDS Humanitarian Services.

The Salt Lake Temple, which took 40 years to build, is one of the most iconic images of the church

A typical meetinghouse of the church, where Sunday worship and social gatherings during the week convene

The Mormon Tabernacle Choir has received a Grammy Award, two Emmy Awards, two Peabody Awards, and the National Medal of Arts.

Interior of the Conference Center where the church holds its General Conferences twice a year

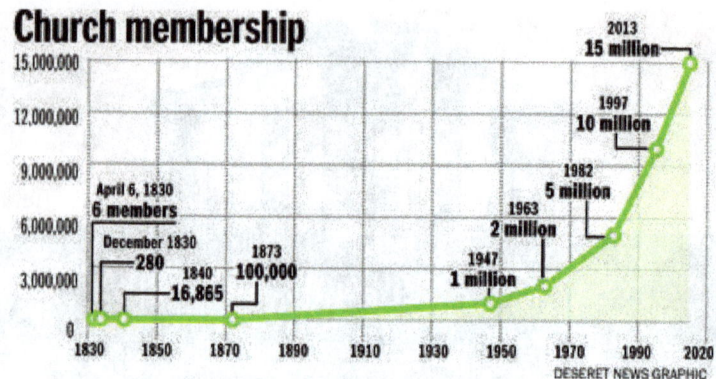

Current membership of the Mormon Church[22]

---

[22]https://mormonchurch.com/3998/fulfilling-prophecy-mormon-church-exponential-growth

Islam

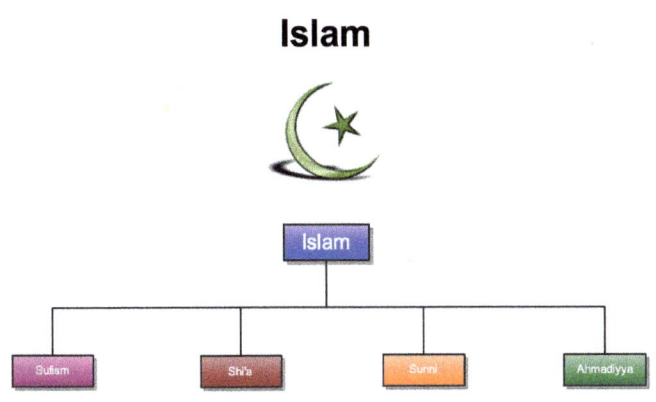

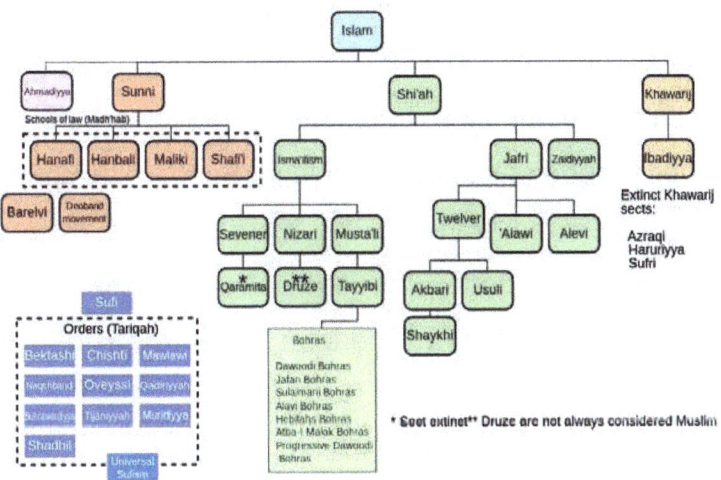

* Sect extinct ** Druze are not always considered Muslim

Islam, founded by Muhammad, whose members worship the God of Jews and Christians. God is called Allah in Arabic and follow the teachings of the Koran. **Islam** means "submission to the will of God"; adherents of **Islam** are called Muslims.[23]

Following Muhammad's[24] death in 632 C.E., the early Muslim community was immediately confronted with the question of who would succeed the prophet as the spiritual and political leader of the community. This was an important issue, since Muhammad had no living male heirs, and left no universally agreed upon successor. The terms for the subsequent and long-lasting divisions of the community, along the lines of proper leadership, are Shi'a and Sunni. The former comes from the Arabic phrase "Shi'at Ali," the "Party of Ali," which supported the leadership of Muhammad's cousin and son-in-law. The term Sunni refers to those

---

[23] http://macaulay.cuny.edu/eportfolios/drabik10website/tools/religion-flow-chart/

[24] http://www.patheos.com/Library/Sunni-Islam/Origins/Beginnings?offset=0&max=1

who did not support Ali's leadership at this crucial juncture, and is also a term derived from an Arabic phrase, "ahl al-sunnawa al-jamaa," the "People of the Prophet's way and Community." While there are subdivisions within each of these two categories, they represent the main sectarian divide among Muslims.

While Sunnism proper would develop legal and theological traditions in subsequent centuries, its origins lie in this original disagreement over who should lead the young Muslim community. It was generally agreed upon that the next leader, or Caliph, should be a member of the prophet's tribe of Quraysh. According to Sunni tradition, an ailing Muhammad designated his long-time companion AbuBakr as his successor when he asked his friend to lead the community in congregational prayer. Traditionally an indication of leadership, the role of leading prayer is thus interpreted by Sunnis as a gesture signifying Abu Bakr as the proper heir to the prophet's authority.

Following Muhammad's death, a group composed of émigrés from Mecca (the Prophet's birthplace) and of Medinans who supported them (called the Ansar, Arabic for helpers, supporters), gathered at a place called Saqifah and chose Abu Bakr as their new leader, eschewing dynastic succession. This type of consensus, called *shura*, was rooted in longstanding methods of communal *arbitration* in the Arabian Peninsula. Later traditions developed, in the wake of this controversial decision, that had the prophet singling Abu Bakr out more explicitly or even naming him in particular, but these are parts of an ongoing dialogue and disagreement with sectarian adversaries who supported other candidates.

These divides were exacerbated and made firm by the conflict and turmoil that continued to plague the Muslim community in its first decades. The First Civil War took place upon the murder of the third Sunni caliph, Uthman. The caliph, of a mixed reputation because of claims of ineffective leadership and nepotism, was besieged in his home and brutally killed. By this time, Ali had succeeded to the caliphate, and

Uthman's supporters accused Ali of failing to avenge his slain predecessor.

For the next five years, the entirety of his reign, Ali faced opposition and revolts. In 656, he faced and defeated an uprising led by one of the prophet's widows, Aisha, and her supporters Talhah and al-Zubayr. This event, dubbed the Battle of the Camel because Aisha herself is said to have ridden into battle in a litter on a camel's back, was not the last obstacle Ali would face. Contenders for power in Syria, relatives of Uthman, faced off in the Battle of Siffin in 658. This prolonged battle came to a close when Muawiya, the leader of the Syrian opposition, had his troops ride into an arbitration with copies of the Quran affixed to the ends of their lances. Ali agreed to arbitration, a fact for which he would pay dearly. Secessionists from his own group of supporters, called Kharijites, betrayed him and declared him an illegitimate leader. Ali was assassinated by a Kharijite in 661.

Summary of Muslim Religion

Population

A comprehensive demographic study of more than 200 countries finds that there are 1.57 billion Muslims living in the world today, representing 23% of an estimated 2009 world population of 6.8 billion.

While Muslims[25] are found on all five continents, more than 60% of the global Muslim population is in Asia and about 20% is in the Middle East and North Africa. However, the Middle East-North Africa region has the highest percentage of Muslim-majority countries. More than half of the 20 countries and territories in that region have populations that are approximately 95% Muslim.

More than 300 million Muslims, or one-fifth of the world's Muslim population, live in countries where Islam is not the majority religion. These minority Muslim

---

[25]http://www.pewresearch.org/fact-tank/2017/02/27/muslims-and-islam-key-findings-in-the-u-s-and-around-the-world/

populations are often quite large. India has the third-largest population of Muslims worldwide. China has more Muslims than Syria, while Russia is home to more Muslims than Jordan and Libya combined.

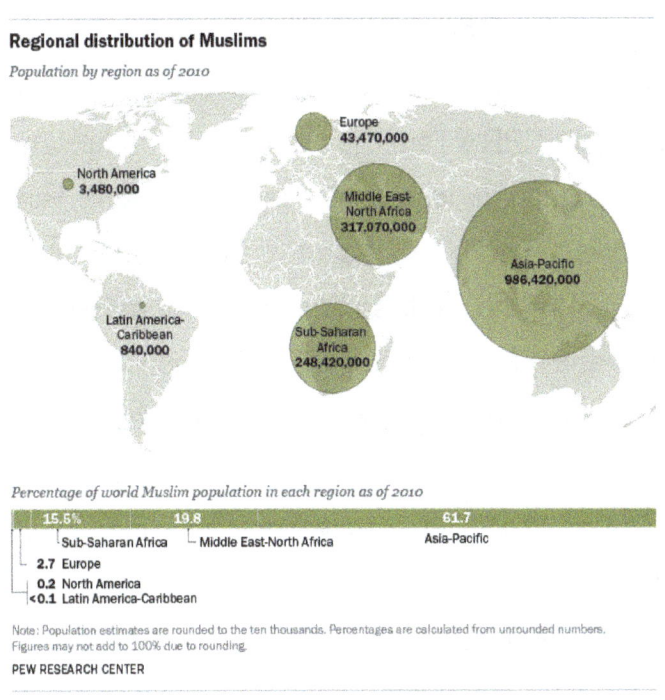

Regional distribution of Muslims

Population by region as of 2010

Percentage of world Muslim population in each region as of 2010

Note: Population estimates are rounded to the ten thousands. Percentages are calculated from unrounded numbers. Figures may not add to 100% due to rounding.

PEW RESEARCH CENTER

Islam is growing more rapidly than any other religion in the world, according to a new report by the

Pew[26] Research Center that says the religion will nearly equal Christianity by 2050 before eclipsing it around 2070.

"The main reason Muslims are growing not only in number but in share worldwide is because of where they live," Alan Cooperman, Pew's director of religion research, tells NPR's Tom Gjelten. "Muslim populations are concentrated in some of the fastest-growing parts of the world." The finding is part of the center's report on the future of the world's religions. You can see the full report at the Pew site, which has also published an interactive tool to help readers drill down by geography and religion.

"As of 2010, Christianity was by far the world's largest religion, with an estimated 2.2 billion adherents, nearly a third (31 percent) of all 6.9 billion people on Earth," the Pew report says. "Islam was second, with 1.6 billion adherents, or 23 percent of the global population." Those numbers are predicted to shift in the

---

[26] http://www.pewforum.org/2013/04/30/the-worlds-muslims-religion-politics-society-overview/

coming decades, as the world's population rises to 9.3 billion by the middle of this century. In that time, Pew projects, Islam will grow by 73 percent while Christianity will grow by 35 percent — resulting in 2.8 billion Muslims and 2.9 billion Christians worldwide.

The report[27] says that by 2050:

- In the U.S., Christianity will decline to claim two-thirds of the population, instead of the more than three-quarters who claimed the religion in 2010.

- Islam will supplant Judaism as the second-most popular religion in the U.S.

- India will displace Indonesia as the home of the world's largest Muslim population, even as the country retains its Hindu majority.

---

[27] http://www.pewforum.org/2013/04/30/the-worlds-muslims-religion-politics-society-overview/

- In addition, Pew says, "Four out of every 10 Christians in the world will live in sub-Saharan Africa."

In addition to presenting raw numbers and projections, the Pew report looks at the demographic trends that are fueling the changes. One factor is the wide range of fertility rates, with only Christians and Muslims currently higher than the world average fertility rate of 2.5

Sufism

The substance of Sufism is the Truth and the meaning of Sufism is the selfless experiencing and actualization of the Truth. The practice of Sufism is the intention to go towards the Truth, by means of love and devotion. This is called the *tarigat*, the spiritual path or way towards God. The sufi is one who is a lover of Truth, who by means of love and devotion moves towards the Truth, towards the perfection which all are truly seeking. As necessitated by love's jealousy, the sufi is taken away from all except the Truth.

Sufism may be traced back as far as the period of Daniel. We find among the Zoroastrians, Hatim, the best known Sufi of his time. The chosen ones of God, the salt of the earth, who responded without hesitation to the call of Abraham, Moses, Jesus and Mohammed, were Sufis, and were not only simple followers of a religion but had insight into divine knowledge. They recognized God's every messenger and united with them all. Before the time of Mohammed they were called Ekuanul Safa, Brothers of Purity, but after his coming they were named by him Sahabi Safa, Knights of Purity. The world has called them Zoroastrian, Christian, Jewish, or Islamic mystics, and the followers of each religion have claimed them as their own. For instance, a Christian would claim that Saint Paul was a Christian and a Muslim that Shams Tabriz was a Muslim. In reality Christ was not a Christian nor was Mohammed a Muslim, they were Sufis.

The word Sufi comes from a Persian word meaning wisdom[28]. From the original root many derivations can be traced; among them the Greek word Sophia is one of the most interesting.

Wisdom is the ultimate power. In wisdom is rooted religion, which connotes law and inspiration. But the point of view of the wise differs from that of the simple followers of a religion. The wise, whatever their faith, have always been able to meet each other beyond those boundaries of external forms and conventions, which are natural and necessary to human life, but which none the less separate humanity.

People of the same thought and point of view are drawn to each other with a tendency to form an exclusive circle. A minority is apt to fence itself off from the crowd. So it has been with the mystics. Mystical ideas are unintelligible to the generality of people. The mystics have, therefore, usually imparted their ideas to a chosen few only, to those whom they could trust, who

---

[28] http://sufiway.org/about-us/the-origins-of-sufism

were ready for initiation and discipleship. Thus great Sufis have appeared at different times and have founded schools of thought. Their expression of wisdom has differed to suit their environments, but their understanding of life has been one and the same. The same herb planted in various atmospheric conditions

The European historian sometimes traces the history of Sufism by noticing the actual occurrence of this word and by referring only to those schools which have definitely wished to be known by this name. Some European scholars find the origin of this philosophy in the teaching of Islam, others connect it with Buddhism. Others do not reject as incredible the Semitic tradition that Sufism's foundation is to be attributed to the teachings of Abraham. But the greater number consider that it arose contemporary to the teaching of Zoroaster. Every age of the world has seen awakened souls, and as it is impossible to limit wisdom to any one period or place, so it is impossible to date the origin of Sufism.

Not only have there been illuminated souls at all times, but there have been times when a wave of illumination has passed over humanity as a whole. The calamity through which the world has lately passed, and the problems of the present difficult situations are due to the existence of boundaries; this fact is already clear to many. Sufism takes away the boundaries which divide different faiths by bringing into full light the underlying wisdom in which they are all united.

Shi'a, a branch is Islam

Shi'a[29] is a branch of Islam which holds that the Islamic prophet Muhammad designated Ali ibn Abi Talib as his successor (Imam). Shia Islam primarily contrasts with Sunni Islam, whose adherents believe that Muhammad did not appoint a successor. Instead they consider Abu Bakr (who was appointed Caliph through a Shura, i.e. consensus) to be the correct Caliph.

Shia Islam is based on the Quran and the message of Muhammad attested in hadith, and on

---

[29]https://en.wikipedia.org/wiki/Shia_Islam

hadith taught by their Imams. Shia consider Ali to have been divinely appointed as the successor to Muhammad, and as the first Imam. The Shia also extend this "Imami" doctrine to Muhammad's family, the Ahl al-Bayt ("the People of the House"), and some individuals among his descendants, known as Imams, who they believe possess special spiritual and political authority over the community, infallibility, and other divinely-ordained traits.

The Shia Islamic faith is vast and inclusive of many different groups. Shia theological beliefs and religious practises, such as prayers, slightly differ from the Sunnis'. While all Muslims pray five times daily, Shias have the option of combining Dhuhr with Asr and Maghrib with Isha', as there are three distinct times mentioned in the Quran. The Sunnis tend to combine only under certain circumstances. Shia Islam embodies a completely independent system of religious interpretation and political authority in the Muslim world. The original Shia identity referred to the followers of Imam Ali and Shia theology was formulated in the 2nd century AH. The first Shia governments and societies were established by the end of the 3rd century AH/9th century CE. Historians dispute the origin of Shia Islam, with many Western scholars positing that Shiism began as a political faction rather than a truly religious movement. Other scholars disagree, considering this concept of religious-political separation to be an anachronistic application of a Western concept.

Sunni Islam

Sunni Islam is the largest Islamic sect.

Formed:	632 CE
Origin:	Middle East
Followers:	940,000,000
Deity:	Allah
Sacred Texts:	Qur'an, Sunnah
Headquarters:	None

In the Sunni sect of Islam, the leader is the Imam, who is the leader of the congregational prayer. In Sunni Islam, the successor of Prophet Muhammad was Abu Bakr, a close companion of the Prophet's. They chose to follow Abu Bakr because they believed he was the best versed in the knowledge of Islam as he learned everything he knew from the Prophet. They also felt that he was the most effective leader. The Sunnis are named so because they believe themselves to follow the sunnah, the traditions of the Prophet.

Sunnis base their religion based on the Quran and the Sunnah as understood by the majority of the community under the structure of four schools of thought. The four schools of thought are the Hanafi, the Maliki, the SHafi'I and the Hanbali. These schools of thoughts are NOT different sects; they are schools of religious law that associate themselves with four great scholars of early Isla,m: Abu Haneehfa, Malik, Shafi'I and Ahmad bin Hanbal. These four scholars were known throughout the Muslim world for their knowledge and piety and only differed in minor issues of application and certain principles in the religion. They were no in opposition to each other. Sunnis regard themselves as the orthodox branch of Islam. The name "Sunni" is derived from the phrase "Ahl al-Sunnah", or "People of the Tradition". The tradition in this case refers to practices based on what the Prophet Muhammad said, did, agreed to or condemned.

All the branches of Sunni Islam testify to six principal articles of faith known as the six pillars of *iman* (Arabic for "faith"), which are believed to be essential for salvation. These are:

- Belief in the One God (see Tawhid)
- Belief in the existence of angels
- Belief in the existence of prophets
- Belief in God's revelations, including
    the Torah (revealedto Moses),
    the Psalms (revealed to David),
    the Gospel (revealed to Jesus), and
    the Quran (revealed to Muhammad)
- Belief in the Day of Judgment

- Belief in God's predestination

Ahmadiyya sect of Islam

The Ahmadiyya sect of Islam is a more radical sect. The distinguishing feature of the Muslim Community is their belief in Mirza Ghulam Ahmad as the Promised Messiah and Mahdi, as prophesied by the Islamic prophet Muhammad. The Islamic world in general is described as follows:

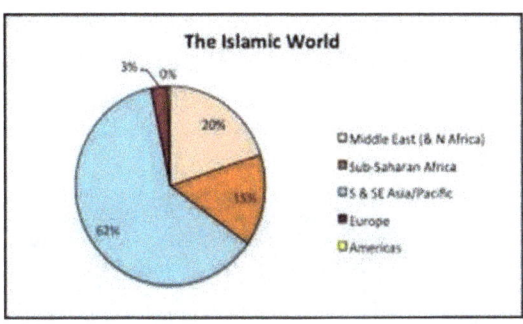

The Imam Hussein Shrine in Karbala, Iraq is a holy site for Shia Muslims.

Dome of the Rock built by Abd al-Malik ibn Marwan; completed at the end of the Second Fitna

Men reading the Quran in a mosque

Muslim men prostrating during prayer in the Umayyad Mosque, Damascus

Judaism

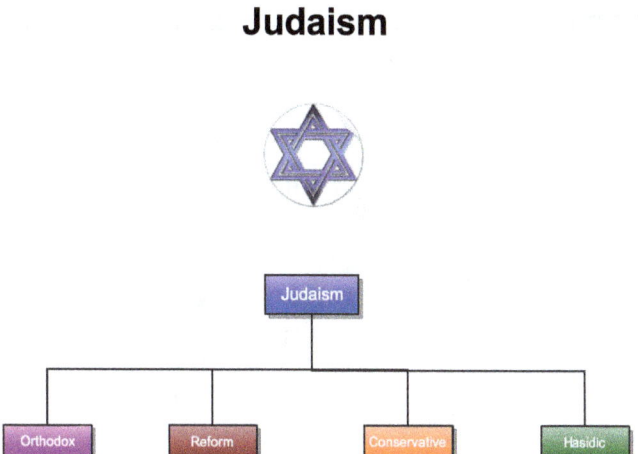

Judaism is an ancient monotheistic religion, with the Torah as its foundational text (part of the larger text known as the Tanakh or Hebrew Bible), and supplemental oral tradition represented by later texts such as the Midrash and the Talmud.[30]

The differences between Jewish denominations are based on the degree that they have rejected or not

---

[30]https://en.wikipedia.org/wiki/Judaism

rejected various aspects of Judaism based on 'modern times'.

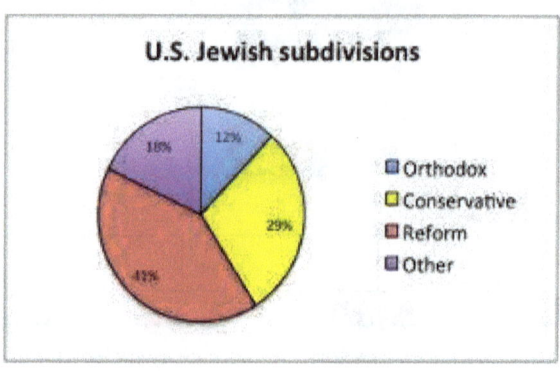

1. Orthodox Judaism

Orthodox Judaism is the most traditional expression of Judaism. Orthodox Jews believe in the entire Torah, including "Written", the Pentateuch, and "Oral", the Talmud. Orthodox Jews reject the changes of all of the various reformist changes to Judaism and believe firmly in the traditional Jewish beliefs and practices. They continue all the traditions of their ancestors, such as the dietary laws, traditional prayers and ceremonies, regular and intensive study of the

Torah, and separation of men and women in the synagogue. Orthodox Jews also strictly observe the Sabbath and religious festivals and do not permit instrumental music during communal services, in memory of the Holy Temple in Jerusalem.

2. Reform Judaism

Reform Judaism is known as the most liberal denomination of Judaism. It is organized under the Union for Reform Judaism in America. Reform Judaism came about in Germany in the early 1800s as a reaction against the perceived severity of Orthodox Judaism as well as a response to Germany's increasing liberal political climate.

Some changes that were made included the de-emphasis on Jews as a united people, the discontinuation of prayers for a return to their historic homeland, prayers and sermons being recited in German instead of Hebrew, the addition of organ music to the synagogue service, and a lack of observance of the dietary laws. However, Modern Reform Judaism has restored some aspects of Judaism that were abandoned in the 19th century. Modern Reform Judaism has included the sense of a Jewish united community, and the practice of some religious rituals.

In Reform Judaism, women may be rabbis, cantors, and synagogue presidents and intermarried families are accepted.

3. Conservative Judaism

Conservative Judaism is a moderate denomination that seeks to avoid the extremes of both, Orthodox and Reform Judaism. Conservative Judaism seeks to conserve the traditional elements of Judaism while also allowing for reasonable modernization and rabbinical development. Conservative Judaism is founded on the teachings of Zacharias Frankel. Frankel insisted that Jewish tradition and rituals were essentials.

Conservative Jews observe the Sabbath and dietary laws, although a few modifications have been made to the latter. Women may also be rabbis. Conservative Jews believe in the importance of Jewish nationalism and they encourage the study of Hebrew. However, beyond these basics, beliefs and practices among the Conservative Jews range from those of Reform to Orthodox.

4. Hasidic Judaism

Hasidic Judaism came about in the 12th-century as a movement that focused on simplicity and mystical experience born out of love and humility before God. The modern Hasidic movement was founded in Poland in the 18th century. It is heavily influenced by the Kabbalah movement and focuses on personal experiences of God instead of religious education and ritual. Modern Hasidic Judaism focuses on the needs of the common people and the Hasidic Jews take the concept that everyday activities are of equivalent importance to religious rituals to an extreme.

The leader in Hasidic Judaism is known as a Rebbe or Tzaddik. A Rebbe does not necessarily have to be ordained. However, the Rebbe is considered especially enlightened and close to God. The Rebbe is looked to for guidance in all aspects of life, from interpreting the Torah to choosing who to marry, or what house to buy. A Rebbe's advice is considered utterly authoritative.

The Jewish People

The Population

Countries with a core Jewish population as of 2013 is 13,854,800. The distributions by countries is as follows:

Israel	6,014,300
USA	5,425,000
France	478,000
Canada	380,000
UK	291,000
Russia	190,000
Argentina	181,500
Germany	181,000

Australia	112,500
Brazil	95,200
South America	70,000
Ukraine	65,000
Hungary	48,000
Mexico	40,000
Belgium	30,000
Netherlands	29,900
Italy	28,100
Chile	18,500

The Jewish population has significant changes since 1948; at that time, Israel (Mandatory Palestine) was less than 1 million, USA was over 4 million and the rest of the people scattered around the world (over 6 million). The Israel-Arab of 1947-48 was a victorious for the Jews and led to the establishment of the State of Israel. Hence, the population of Jews grow from less than 1 million to the present state over 6 million.

The Religion

The Jewish people has the ascent religion of one God (monotheistic religion) or Judaism with the Torah as its fundamental text. Judaism is considered by religious Jews to be the expression of the covenantal relationship that God established with the Children of Israel.

Within Judaism there are a variety of movements, which holds that God revealed his laws and commandments to Moses on Mount Sinai in the form of both the Written and Oral Torah. Historically, this assertion was challenged by various groups during the early and later medieval period; and among segments of the modern non-Orthodox denominations.

Modern branches of Judaism. Today, the largest Jewish religious movements are Orthodox Judaism and Modern Orthodox Judaism), Conservative Judaism and Reform Judaism. Major sources of difference between these groups are their approaches to Jewish law. Orthodox Judaism maintains that the Torah and Jewish law are divine in origin, eternal and unalterable, and that they should be strictly followed. Conservative and Reform Judaism are more liberal, with Conservative Judaism generally promoting a more "traditional" interpretation of Judaism's requirements than Reform Judaism. A typical Reform position is that Jewish law should be viewed as a set of general guidelines rather than as a set of restrictions and obligations whose observance is required of all Jews. Historically, special courts enforced Jewish law, but today, these courts still exist but the practice of Judaism is mostly voluntary. Authority on theological and legal matters is not vested in any one person or organization, but in the sacred texts and rabbis and scholars who interpret them. The history of Judaism spans more than 3,000 years.

Judaism has its roots as a structured religion in the Middle East during the Bronze Age. Judaism is considered one of the oldest monotheistic religions. Jews are an ethnoreligious group and include those born Jewish and converts to Judaism. In 2015, the world Jewish population was estimated at about 14.3 million, or roughly 0.2% of the total world population. About 43% of all Jews reside in Israel and another 43% reside in the United States and Canada, with most of the remainder living in Europe, and other minority groups spread throughout South America, Asia, Africa, and Australia

The Western Wall, in the Old City of Jerusalem, all that remains of the Second Temple.

An orthodox jews prayer

The portion of a synagogue where prayer is performed is called the sanctuary.

Hinduism

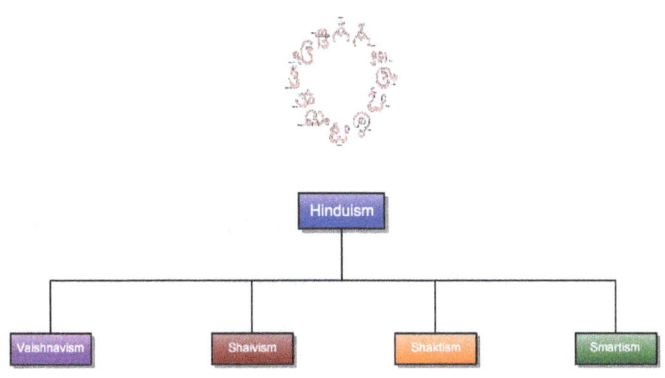

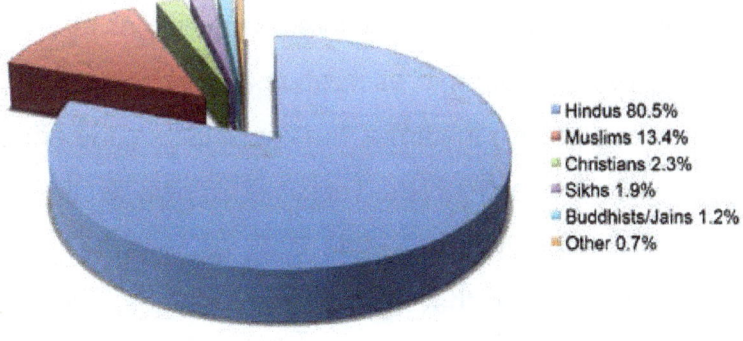

The following nine beliefs, though not exhaustive, offer a simple summary of Hindu spirituality[31].

1. Hindus believe in a one, all-pervasive Supreme Being who is both immanent and transcendent, both Creator and Unmanifest Reality.
2. Hindus believe in the divinity of the four Vedas, the world's most ancient scripture, and venerate the Agamas as equally revealed. These primordial hymns are God's word and the bedrock of Sanatana Dharma, the eternal religion.
3. Hindus believe that the universe undergoes endless cycles of creation, preservation and dissolution.
4. Hindus believe in karma, the law of cause and effect by which each individual creates his own destiny by his thoughts, words and deeds.
5. Hindus believe that the soul reincarnates, evolving through many births until all karmas have been

---

[31]https://www.himalayanacademy.com/readlearn/basics/nine-beliefs

resolved, and moksha, liberation from the cycle of rebirth, is attained. Not a single soul will be deprived of this destiny.

6. Hindus believe that divine beings exist in unseen worlds and that temple worship, rituals, sacraments and personal devotionals create a communion with these devas and Gods.

7. Hindus believe that an enlightened master, or satguru, is essential to know the Transcendent Absolute, as are personal discipline, good conduct, purification, pilgrimage, self-inquiry, meditation and surrender in God.

8. Hindus believe that all life is sacred, to be loved and revered, and therefore practice ahimsa, non-injury, in thought, word and deed.

9. Hindus believe that no religion teaches the only way to salvation above all others, but that all genuine paths are facets of God's Light, deserving tolerance and understanding.

The four facts--karma, reincarnation, all-pervasive divinity and dharma--are the essence of the Vedas and Agamas and the fabric of every Hindu's life. Speak of them to all who will listen. They are the heritage of all souls.

KARMA

According as one acts, so does he Become. One becomes virtuous by virtuous action, bad by bad action. Yajur Veda, Brihadaranyaka Upanishad.

Karma literally means "deed" or "act" and more broadly names the universal principle of cause and effect, action and reaction which governs all life. Karma is a natural law of the mind, just as gravity is a law of matter. Karma is not fate, for man acts with free will, creating his own destiny. The Vedas tell us, if we sow goodness, we will reap goodness; if we sow evil, we will reap evil. Karma refers to the totality of our actions and their concomitant reactions in this and previous lives, all of which determines our future. It is the interplay between our experience and how we respond to it that makes karma devastating or helpfully invigorating. The conquest of karma lies in intelligent action and dispassionate reaction. Not all karmas rebound immediately. Some accumulate and return unexpectedly in this or other births.

REINCARNATION

After death, the soul goes to the next world, bearing in mind the subtle impressions of its deeds, and after reaping their harvest returns again to this world of action. Thus, he who has desires continues subject to rebirth.

Reincarnation, punarjanma, is the natural process of birth, death and rebirth. At death we drop off the physical body and continue evolving in the inner worlds in our subtle bodies, until we again enter into birth. Through the ages, reincarnation has been the great consoling element within Hinduism, eliminating the fear of death. We are not the body in which we live but the immortal soul which inhabits many bodies in its evolutionary journey through samsara. After death, we continue to exist in unseen worlds, enjoying or suffering the harvest of earthly deeds until it comes time for yet another physical birth. The actions set in motion in previous lives form the tendencies and conditions of the next. Reincarnation ceases when karma is resolved, God is realized and moksha, liberation, is attained.

ALL-PERVASIVE DIVINITY

He is the God of forms infinite in whose glory all things are--smaller than the smallest atom, and yet the Creator of all, ever living in the mystery of His creation. In the vision of this God of love there is everlasting peace. He is the Lord of all who, hidden in the heart of things, watches over the world of time.

As a family of faiths, Hinduism upholds a wide array of perspectives on the Divine, yet all worship the one, all-pervasive Supreme Being hailed in the Upanishads. As Absolute Reality, God is unmanifest, unchanging and transcendent, the Self God, timeless, formless and spaceless. As Pure Consciousness, God is the manifest primal substance, pure love and light flowing through all form, existing everywhere in time and space as infinite intelligence and power. As Primal Soul, God is our personal Lord, source of all three worlds, our Father-Mother God who protects, nurtures and guides us. We beseech God's grace in our lives while also knowing that He/She is the essence of our soul, the life of our life. Each denomination also venerates its own pantheon of Divinities, Mahadevas, or "great angels," who were created by the Supreme Lord and who serve and adore Him.

DHARMA

Dharma yields Heaven's honor and Earth's wealth. What is there then that is more fruitful for a man? There is nothing more rewarding than dharma, nor anything more ruinous than its neglect.

When God created the universe, He endowed it with order, with the laws to govern creation. Dharma is God's divine law prevailing on every level of existence, from the sustaining cosmic order to religious and moral laws which bind us in harmony with that order. Related to the soul, dharma is the mode of conduct most conducive to spiritual advancement, the right and righteous path. It is piety and ethical practice, duty and obligation. When we follow dharma, we are in conformity with the Truth that inheres and instructs the universe, and we naturally abide in closeness to God. Adharma is opposition to divine law. Dharma is to the individual what its normal development is to a seed--the orderly fulfillment of an inherent nature and destiny.

There are six schools of philosophy in Hinduism known as: Nyaya, Vaisheshika, Samkhya, Yoga, PurvaMimasa and Uttara Mimasa. These six schools of philosophy are incorporated into all the different denominations of Hinduism. There are also numerous sects and numerous sacred books. The major sects of Hinduism are the following:

1. Vaishnavism

Vaishnavism is regarded as a monotheistic sect. Vaishnavism has a belief in one supreme God known as Vishnu. The Supreme God simultaneously infuses all creation. However, there are also many lower Gods under the Supreme One. Vishnu encompasses these gods. The main belief of Vaishnavism is that there is an emphasis on God as a personal being. Vaishnavites believe that God is someone you can know and have a relationship with. They believe that the six qualities of God include all knowledge, all power, supreme majesty, supreme strength, unlimited energy and total self-sufficiency.

Vaishnavism is the largest sect. Vaishnava texts include the Vedas as well as the Bhagavad Gita, the BhagavataPurana, the Vishnu Samhita, and the Gita Govinda.

Vaishnavites recognize the importance of meditation in religious practice. Vaishnavites believe that it is more important to believe and to be devout than to study the doctrines and focus on religious knowledge.

2. Shaivism

Shaivism is regarded as a monotheistic sect. Shaivism has a belief in one supreme God known as Shiva. Shaivites believe that the entire creation is an expression of conscious divinity and is no different from the divinity, which they call Shiva because he is both the created and the creator. This concept differs from many other religions that see God as fundamentally different from the creation and is considered higher. Shaivism also acknowledges the existence of many other deities.

3. Shaktism

Shaktism focuses worship upon Shakti or Devi, the Hindu Divine Mother. Shakti doctrine tends to emphasize the non-difference between matter and spirit, and looks to the creative force of matter rather than its ability to delude and entangle. For this reason, Shaktas worship for material benefit as well as final liberation. A notable aspect of Shaktism is animal sacrifice and even documented accounts of human sacrifice.

4. Smartism

Smartism refers to those who follow the Vedas and Shastras (religious texts). Believers of Smartism mainly follow the Advaita Vedanta philosophy of AdiShankara, who bases his teachings on the unity of the soul and Brahman. Smartas believe that the worshipper is free to choose a particular aspect of God to worship.

Akshardham, one of the largest Hindu temples in the world[32]

Palitana Jain Temples.

---

[32]https://en.wikipedia.org/wiki/Religion_in_India

A temple in rural South India September 2013

The DAKHSHINESWAR TEMPLE was founded by RANI (Queen) of Janbaazar RASHMONI in 1855 on the east bank of the Ganges River.

Hindues worship the son God at Sangam during Chhath festival in Allahabad

Happy Diwali and Surasamharam-2[33]

---

[33] http://www.gurusfeet.com/blog/happy-diwali-and-surasamharam-2

Chinese Religion

China[34] has been a multi-religion country since the ancient times. It is well known that Confucianism is an indigenous religion and is the soul of Chinese culture. It became the guiding ideology for feudalism society, but it did not develop into a national belief. It makes the culture more tolerant to others, thus, many other religions have been brought into the country in different dynasties, but none of them developed powerful enough in the history and they only provide diverse people more spiritual support.

According to a latest survey, 85% of Chinese people have religious beliefs or had some religious practices and only 15% of them are real atheists. The real atheists here refer to those who lack belief in the existence of deities and do not join in any religious activities. 185 million people believe in Buddhism and 33 million have faith in Christianity and believes in the

---

[34]https://www.travelchinaguide.com/intro/religion/

existence of God. Only 12 million people are Taoists, although more than one hundred million have taken part in Taoism activities before. Thus, it is obvious that the Buddhism has the widest influence. The other major religions are Taoism, Confucianism, Islam and Christianity.

Buddhism

Being brought into China 2,000 years ago, it was gradually widely accepted by most Chinese people and developed into three sections, namely the Han, Tibetan and Southern Buddhism. Buddhism not only brought a different religion, but also brought a different culture. It influences the local culture on three main aspects: literature, art and ideology. Many famous poems have ideas from Buddhism and many Buddhist stone statues can be found, which show its huge influence. It also promotes the countries' intercultural communications with foreign countries. In Tang Dynasty (618 - 907), Jianzhen traveled to Japan to spread Buddhism as well as Chinese culture. Xuanzang, who traveled to India to learn Buddhist doctrines, brought a plenty information on the language of the countries he had been to.

Now, Buddhism has developed into the most important religion in the country. The latest survey shows that 31% of the people who do not believe in this religion have participated in some Buddhist activities and about 17 million people have already become converts. Now more of those followers come from different walks of life such as the intellectuals, business elites and the common people. Recently, there is a new report, The Chinese Luxury Consumer White Paper 2012, jointly published by the Industrial Bank and Hurun Report, which shows that 39% of the intellectuals and businessmen have faith in Buddhism. Not only the number of the followers is increasing, and the education of Buddhism obtains more attention from the society. Under the Buddhist Association of China, 34 different levels of Buddhist academies as well as almost 50 magazines can be found. Now in mainland China, there are about 13 thousand temples and 180 thousand monks and nuns.

Han Buddhism: With 8,400 temples and 50 thousand monks, it is the largest branch on the mainland.

Tibetan Buddhism: As the second large sect, it has 3,000 temples and 120 thousand monks.

Southern Buddhism: Having 8,000 monks and 1,600 temples, this sect has the smallest scale.

Confucianism

Confucianism, not a real religion, is just an ethical and philosophical system, which developed from Confucius' thoughts and later was treated as a kind of belief to educate common people. It obtained its stable position under the reign of Emperor Wu of Han Dynasty (202BC-220AD), and became the ideology of the society in the feudal system since then. Based on the Four Books and Five Classics, the traditions and principles in the Confucianism played an important role in the formation of Chinese people's thinking patterns and teaching methods. For instance, Doctrine of the Mean can be seen on communications among people.

Now, to some extent, where Chinese people stay or live, there will be Confucianism.

Confucianism has worldwide influence. In many countries and regions of world such the UK, USA, branches of Confucius Institutes are established in recent years to spread Chinese culture and expand the language. In China, you can find many Confucius temples, which is an important place for the candidates for important exams. In Beijing, They hang some red wooden plates with lucky words in the Confucius Temple in the hope of gaining high marks and a good future.

Taoism

Taoism, with more than 1,800 years' history originated in the Warring Period and came into being in Eastern Han Dynasty (25 - 220). Now about 300 Taoist Temples are scattered around China, in which about 30 thousand Taoists lived in. Around 5 Taoist schools exist in the country and two main sections are included in Taoism. In the 1,800 years, Taoism influenced the local culture deeply, especially on traditional medicine and literature. Based on some theories of alchemists such as Wei Boyang in Eastern Han Dynasty, different kinds of medicine prescriptions were created by Sun Simiao and many other doctors. In literature, many fictional characters are closely related with Taoism, such as the Jade Emperor. Apart from Mainland China, many Taoists live in Hong Kong, Macau and some foreign countries.

Islam

Being introduced into China in the 7th century in Tang Dynasty, Islam has more than 1,400 years' history in the country. Now, Muslims live everywhere, but the highest concentrations are Ningxia Hui Autonosmous Region, Xinjiang Uygur Autonomous Region, Gansu Province and even Qinghai Province. Sunni Islam was the main branch worshipped by almost all the Muslims in the country.

Christianity

Christianity was first introduced to China in Tang Dynasty, which was named as Nestorianism during that time. After 1840, they swept the country. Although they were suspended after 1949, it spread fast in recent years. Now about 30 million Chinese people are Christians, who are organized in about 97 parishes. Most of Christians gather in the south part of the country.

Other beliefs

In addition to the five main religions, Chinese people have some other traditional folk beliefs. More than 200 million people believe the existence of the ancestors' souls and worship them, while about 700 million have taken part in the activities to worship their ancestors or related activities. About 150 million people believe in Fengshui theory and 140 million people believe in God of Wealth. Chinese Astrology is very popular and many people think the sign can decide one's characters and future. Thus, it is obvious that the traditional folk belief has a wide foundation among the local people. Now, more and more Chinese people are fond of constellation in western culture. In the beginning of a new year, some people will watch some fortune telling programs to see whether they can succeed in the next year and learn how to avoid back luck.

Brahma Palace of the Buddhist Vatican in Wuxi, Jiangsu, mainland China, has become a focus of Chinese Buddhist and other East Asian Buddhist schools.

Traditional Buddhist ceremony in Hangzhou, Zhejiang province, China[35]

A Temple of the God of Culture in Liuzhou, Guangxi, where Confucius is worshiped as *Wéndì* "God of Culture

---

[35]ps://en.wikipedia.org/wiki/Chinese_Buddhism#/media/File:Chinese_Buddhist_Monks_Ceremony_Hangzhou.jpeg

Legislator Regina Ip Lau Suk-yee, president of the Confucian Academy Dr Tong Yun-kai and then Executive Council convenor Leung Chun-ying officiate a ceremony to celebrate Confucius' 2,562nd birthday, at the Queen Elizabeth Stadium, in Wan Chai, on September 24, 2011

Taoist rite at the Qingyanggong (Green Goat Temple) in Chengdu

Priests of the Zhengyi order bowing while officiating a rite at the White Cloud Temple of Shanghai[36]

St. Dominic's Church in Macau is one of the oldest (AD 1587) existing churches in China built by three Spanish Dominican priests[37].

---

[36]https://en.wikipedia.org/wiki/Taoism
[37]https://en.wikipedia.org/wiki/Christianity_in_China

Christian congregations in particular have skyrocketed since churches began reopening when Chairman Mao's death in 1976

The Buddhist Religion

Buddhism arose in northeastern India sometime between the late 6th century and the early 4th century, a period of great social change and intense religious activity. There is disagreement among scholars about the dates of the Buddha's birth and death. Many modern scholars believe that the historical Buddha lived from about 563 to about 483. Many others believe that he lived about 100 years later (from about 448 to 368). At this time in India, there was much discontent with Brahmanic (Hindu high-caste) sacrifice and ritual. In northwestern India there were ascetics who tried to create a more personal and spiritual religious experience than that found in the Vedas (Hindu sacred scriptures). In the literature that grew out of this movement, the Upanishads, a new emphasis on renunciation and transcendental knowledge can be found. Northeastern India, which was less influenced by Vedic tradition, became the breeding ground of many new sects. Society in this area was troubled by the breakdown of tribal unity and the expansion of several petty kingdoms. Religiously, this was a time of doubt, turmoil, and experimentation.[38]

In general, Buddhism is a way of finding peace within oneself. It is a religion that helps us to find the happiness and contentment we seek. Buddhists develop inner peace, kindness and wisdom through their daily practice; and then share their experience with others bringing real benefit to this world. They try not to harm others and to live peacefully and gently, working towards the ultimate goal of pure and lasting happiness for all living beings. The evidence of the early texts suggests that he was born as Siddhārtha Gautama in Lumbini and grew up in Kapilavatthu, a town in the plains region of modern Nepal-India border, and that he spent his life in what is now modern Bihar and Uttar Pradesh. Some hagiographic legends state that his father was a king named Suddhodana, his mother queen Maya, and he was born in Lumbini gardens.[39]

---

[38]https://www.britannica.com/topic/Buddhism
[39]http://www.aboutbuddhism.org/

Early Buddhist canonical texts and early biographies of Buddha state that Gautama studied under Vedic teachers, such as Alara Kalama (Sanskrit: Arada Kalama) and UddakaRamaputta (Sanskrit: UdrakaRamaputra), learning meditation and ancient philosophies, particularly the concept of "nothingness, emptiness" from the former, and "what is neither seen nor unseen" from the latte. There are 376 million followers worldwide.

A wide range of meditation practices has developed in the Buddhist traditions, but "meditation" primarily refers to the practice of dhyanac.q. jhana. It is a practice in which the attention of the mind is first narrowed to the focus on one specific object, such as the breath, a concrete object, or a specific thought, mental image or mantra. After this initial focussing of the mind, the focus is coupled to mindfulness, maintaining a calm mind while being aware of one's surroundings. The practice of dhyana aids in maintaining a calm mind, and avoiding disturbance of this calm mind by mindfulness of disturbing thoughts and feeling.[40]

Key facts

- Buddhism is 2,500 years old
- There are currently 376 million followers worldwide
- There are over 150,000 Buddhists in Britain
- Buddhism arose as a result of Siddhartha Gautama's quest for Enlightenment in around the 6th Century BC
- There is no belief in a personal God. It is not centred on the relationship between humanity and God
- Buddhists believe that nothing is fixed or permanent - change is always possible
- The two main Buddhist
  - ➢ sectare Theravada Buddhism
  - ➢ and Mahayana Buddhism,

---

[40]https://en.wikipedia.org/wiki/Buddhism

- Buddhists can worship both at home or at a temple
- The path to Enlightenment is through the practice and development of morality, meditation and wisdom.

The Dalai Lama

The Dalai Lama is the head monk of Tibetan Buddhism and traditionally has been responsible for the governing of Tibet, until the Chinese government took control in 1959. Before 1959, his official residence was Potala Palace in Lhasa, the capital of Tibet.

The Dalai Lama belongs to the Gelugpa tradition of Tibetan Buddhism, which is the largest and most influential tradition in Tibet. The institution of the Dalai Lama is a relatively recent one. There have been only 14 Dalai Lamas in the history of Buddhism, and the first and second Dalai Lamas were given the title posthumously.

According to Buddhist belief, the current Dalai Lama is a reincarnation of a past lama who decided to be reborn again to continue his important work, instead of moving on from the wheel of life. A person who decides to be continually reborn is known as *tulku*. Buddhists believe that the first tulku in this reincarnation was Gedun Drub, who lived from 1391-1474 and the second was GendunGyatso. However, the name Dalai Lama, meaning Ocean of Wisdom, was not conferred until the third reincarnation in the form of SonamGyatso in 1578.

The current Dalai Lama is Tenzin Gyatso.

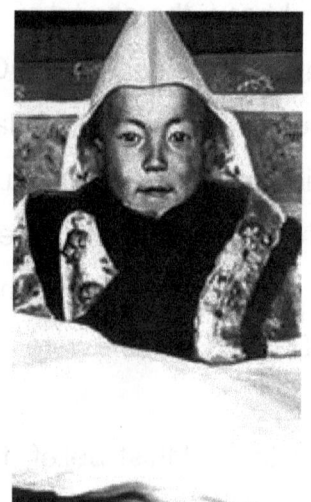

Tenzin Gyatso, 14th Dalai Lama, as a child.

Choosing a Dalai Lama.

After the death of a Dalai Lama it has traditionally been the responsibility of the High Lamas of the Gelugpa Tradition and the Tibetan government to find his reincarnation. The High Lamas search for a boy who was born around the same time as the death of the Dalai Lama. It can take around two or three years to identify the Dalai Lama, and for the current, 14th Dalai Lama, it was four years before he was found.

There are several ways in which the High Lamas might find out where the next reincarnation will be found.

- Dream
  - One of the High Lamas may dream about some mark or location that will identify the boy.
- Smoke

- If the previous Dalai Lama was cremated, High Lamas will watch the direction of the smoke and search accordingly.
- Oracle Lake
  - High Lamas go to a holy lake, called LhamoLhatso, in central Tibet and watch for a sign from the lake itself. This may be either a vision or some indication of the direction in which to search. The home and village of Tenzin Gyatso was identified in a vision from this lake.

Once the High Lamas have located the home and the boy, they present a number of artefacts which they have brought with them in preparation, to the child. Amongst these artefacts are a number of items that belonged to the deceased Dalai Lama. If the boy chooses the items that belonged to the previous Dalai Lama, this is seen as a sign, in conjunction with all of the other indications, that the boy is a reincarnation.

This procedure, however, as Tenzin Gyatso has said himself, is not set in stone; if two thirds of the

Tibetan people wish to change the method of identifying the next reincarnation, this would be just as valid.

The search for the Dalai Lama has usually been limited to Tibet, although the third *tulku* was born in Mongolia. However, as Tibet has been taken by the Chinese government, Tenzin Gyatso says that if he is reborn it will not be in a country run by the People's Republic of China, or any other country which is not free.

In 1989 he received the Nobel Peace Prize for maintaining a policy of non-violence with the Chinese government, despite the knowledge that many Tibetans would be happy to take up armed resistance to return him to his position as their leader[41].

---

[41] http://www.bbc.co.uk/religion/religions/buddhism/people/dalailama_1.shtml

Potala Palace, the Dalai Lama's residence until 1959

Dhamek Stupa in Sarnath, India, where the Buddha gave his first sermon. It was built by Ashoka.

Bhikkhus in Thailand[42]

Monks debating at Sera Monastery, Tibet

---

[42]https://en.wikipedia.org/wiki/Buddhism

More details
Bhatti (devotion) at a Buddhist temple, Tibet. Chanting during Bhatti Puja (devotional worship) is often a part of the Theravada Buddhist tradition

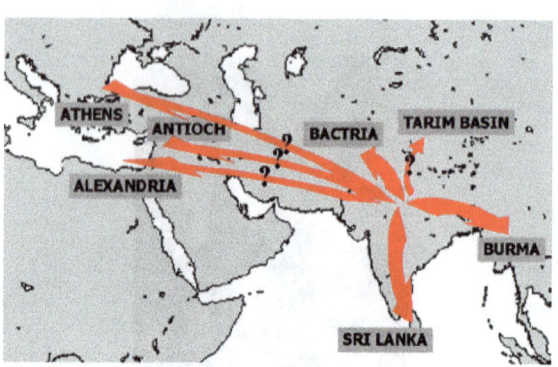

The spread of Buddhism at the time of emperor Ashoka (260–218 BCE

Sikhism religion

There are 20 million Sikhs in the world, most of whom live in the Punjab province of India. The 2001 census recorded 336,000 Sikhs in the UK.

Sikhism was founded in the 16th century in the Punjab district of what is now India and Pakistan. It was founded by Guru Nanak and is based on his teachings, and those of the 9 Sikh gurus who followed him. Guru Nanak (1469-1539) was one of the greatest religious innovators of all time and the founder of the Sikh religion. Nanak's religious ideas draw on both Hindu and Islamic thought, but are far more than just a synthesis. Nanak was an original spiritual thinker and expressed his thoughts in extraordinary poetry that forms the basis of Sikh scripture.

The most important thing in Sikhism is the internal religious state of the individual.

- Sikhism is a monotheistic religion

- Sikhism stresses the importance of doing good actions rather than merely carrying out rituals
- Sikhs believe that the way to lead a good life is to:
  - keep God in heart and mind at all times
  - live honestly and work hard
  - treat everyone equally
  - be generous to the less fortunate
  - serve others
- The Sikh place of worship is called a Gurdwara (a place to worship as a Sikh).

The Sikh scripture is the Guru Granth Sahib, a book that Sikhs consider a living Guru[43].

- There is only one God
- God is without form, or gender
- Everyone has direct access to God
- Everyone is equal before God

---

[43] http://www.bbc.co.uk/religion/religions/sikhism/ataglance/glance.shtml

- A good life is lived as part of a community, by living honestly and caring for others
- Empty religious rituals and superstitions have no value
- Living in God and community

Sikhs focus their lives around their relationship with God, and being a part of the Sikh community. The Sikh ideal combines action and belief. To live a good life a person should do good deeds as well as meditating on God.

Sikhism and abortion

Abortion is generally forbidden in Sikhism, as it interferes in the creative work of God - who created everything and is present in every being.

Most Sikhs accept that life begins at conception (one reference is found on page 74 of the Guru Granth Sahib). So if conception has taken place, it would be a sin to destroy life and hence deliberate miscarriage or abortion is forbidden. The Sikh code of conduct does not deal with abortion (or indeed many other bioethical issues). Despite this theoretical viewpoint, abortion is not uncommon among the Sikh community in India, and there is concern that the practice of aborting female embryos because of a cultural preference for sons is growing.

Sikh moral thinking

Sikhs derive their ethics largely from the teachings of their scripture, Guru Granth Sahib, and the Sikh Code of Conduct (the RehatMaryada). Guidance also comes from the example set by the gurus, and from the experience of the Sikh community over the last 500 years. These do not give detailed answers to many ethical questions, but rather set down general principles and provide a framework for Sikhs to answer those questions.

Sikhs have a high respect for life which they see as a gift from God. Most Sikhs are against euthanasia, as they believe that the timing of birth and death should be left in God's hands. The Sikh Gurus rejected suicide (and by extension, euthanasia) as an interference in God's plan. Suffering, they said, was part of the operation of karma, and human beings should not only accept it without complaint but act so as to make the best of the situation that karma has given them.

DharamYudh - Just War

Sikhism has a concept of the Just War. It's called *DharamYudh*, meaning war in the defence of righteousness.

In such a war:

- the war must be the last resort - all other ways of resolving the conflict must be tried first
- the motive must not be revenge or enmity
- the army must not include mercenaries
- the army must be disciplined
- only the minimum force needed for success should be used
- civilians must not be harmed

- there must be no looting, territory must not be annexed, property taken must be returned

Sikhism and birth control

Sikhs have no objection to birth control. Whether or not Sikhs use contraception, and the form of contraception used, is a matter for the couple concerned.

Sikhism and organ donation

Sikhs have no objections to the donation and transplantation of organs. Sikh philosophy and teachings place great emphasis on the importance of giving and putting others before oneself. Sikh teachings also stress the importance of noble deeds, selfless giving and sacrifice. This is exemplified by the behaviour of the ten Gurus in the Sikh teachings. Saving a human life is one of the greatest things one can do according to the Sikh religion. For this reason, donating organs after death is acceptable to Sikhs.

Sikhs believe in life after death, and a continuous cycle of rebirth. But the physical body is not needed in this cycle. The soul of a person is eternal, but the body is simply flesh and perishable. If another person can make use of organs from a Sikh's body, this is a good thing[44].

The Golden Temple, or Harmandir Sahib, in Amritsar, Punjab, northwestern India.

---

[44]https://www.britannica.com/topic/Sikhism

The Gurudwara Bangla Sahib, a Sikh house of worship dedicated to the eighth Sikh Guru, Hari

Spiritualist church

A spiritualist church is a church affiliated with the informal spiritualist movement which began in the United States in the 1840s. Spiritualist churches are now found around the world, but are most common in English-speaking countries, while in Latin America, where a form of spiritualism called spiritism is more popular, meetings are held in spiritist centres, most of which are non-profit organizations rather than ecclesiastica.

There are Spiritualist churches in Australia, New Zealand, Canada, The Republic of South Africa, Sweden and groups in many countries including Japan, the Scandinavian countries, Korea, Italy, Germany, Austria, Hungary, The Netherlands, Belgium, Spain, Portugal and Iceland. Many such groups and also individuals, are members of the International Spiritualist Federation (ISF) which was founded in Belgium in 1923 and is an umbrella organization for all spiritualists. The ISF holds congresses every two years in different parts of the world.

In Australia, the Associated Christian Spiritual Churches of Australia (ACSCOA) and the Victorian Spiritualists' Union (VSU) co-exist alongside independent churches, and Canada has the Spiritualist Church of Canada (SCC) founded in 1974, along with a number of independent churches[45].

The spiritualist church is to build a thriving spiritual community which supports individuals' personal and spiritual growth through worship services, workshops, training programs and pastoral leadership; and to conduct worship services that may include meditation, healing discourse and spirit communication.

By promoting spiritual self-development, they are offering classes, workshops and training. To provide spiritual healing to those who request it, with the understanding that this does not replace a

---

[45] https://en.wikipedia.org/wiki/Spiritualist_church

physician's medical care. To perform spiritual marriage blessings, memorial services and naming ceremonies to those who desire a more spiritual environment for major life events.

They are a sacred gathering place where everyone can join tighter to share, learn, heal, serve and build a thriving diverse spiritual community that expresses the indwelling source Energy that we call God. They believe that we are all One in Spirit, and as Spirit, we are eternal beings. We accept that as part of Source Energy that we call God, love is our natural state, and living joyfully and abundantly is our birthright.

We affirm that by applying the principles of Universal Law, we can obtain self-mastery, and through unconditional love can be at peace with ourselves and others[46]

Spiritual Healing can be used with other therapies or healing modalities, as well as with conventional medicine. In fact, healers in Britain now

---

[46] http://www.ottawaspiritualpathways.com

have access to hospitals and clinics and work alongside physicians. Some individuals in Canada offer their services to seniors' groups, cancer and pain clinics and to hospices. Healers, however, may not diagnose, interfere with medical treatments or promise definite results.

Founded in Ottawa in 2012, OSPC is a charitable not-for-profit organization whose healing ministry is patterned after the British *Natural Federation of Spiritual Healers (NFSH)*. Operating with a Board, and a strict Healers Code of Conduct and Protocols for Healing in Public. OSPC offers Spiritual Healing Classes as well as an Intuitive Development program and a five-year Ministry Program.

Spiritualism is a way of life. It combines philosophy, science and religion. Spiritualists agree on seven principles:

1. A Divine Intelligence recognized as God.
2. The unity of all life.
3. Divine guidance and inspiration available to every soul.

4. The continuous existence of every soul.
5. Personal responsibility for all thoughts, words and deeds.
6. All of our actions create our environment in this world and the next.
7. Eternal progress is open to every soul[47].

A church in Victoria, B.C.

---

[47] http://cowichanspiritualistchurch.com/contact_us.html

Some members of the congregation[48]

Members of the congregation.

---

[48]https://www.firstspiritualists.com/photo-gallery/

Baha'i religion

Three core principles establish a basis for Bahá'í teachings and doctrine: the unity of God, the unity of religion, and the unity of humanity. From these postulates stems the belief that God periodically reveals his will through divine messengers, whose purpose is to transform the character of humankind and to develop, within those who respond, moral and spiritual qualities. Religion is thus seen as orderly, unified, and progressive from age to age[49]

MírzáHusayn `AlíNúrí was one of the early followers of the Báb, and later took the title of Bahá'u'lláh. He was arrested and imprisoned in 1852 for his involvement with the Bábi movement. Shortly thereafter he was expelled from Tehran to Baghdad, in the Ottoman Empire; then to Constantinople (now Istanbul); and then to Adrianople (now Edirne). In 1863, at the time of his banishment from Baghdad to Constantinople, Bahá'u'lláh declared his claim to a

---

[49]https://en.wikipedia.org/wiki/Bah%C3%A1'%C3%AD_Faith

divine mission to his family and followers. Tensions then grew between him and Subh-i-Azal, the appointed leader of the Bábís who did not recognize Bahá'u'lláh's claim. Throughout the rest of his life Bahá'u'lláh gained the allegiance of most of the Bábís, who came to be known as Bahá'ís. Beginning in 1866, he began declaring his mission as a Messenger of God in letters to the world's religious and secular rulers, including Pope Pius IX, Napoleon III, and Queen Victoria.

The following principles are frequently listed as a quick summary of the Bahá'í teachings. They are derived from transcripts of speeches given by `Abdu'l-Bahá during his tour of Europe and North America in 1912.The list is not authoritative and a variety of such lists circulate.

- Unity of God: I essentially monolithic, defined as the belief in the existence of only one god that created the world,

- Unity of religion: is a core teaching of the Bahá'í Faith which states that there is a fundamental unity in many of the world's religions.
- Unity of humanity: state that since all humans have been created in the image of God, God does not make any distinction between people regardlessof race or colour.
- Unity in diversity: unity in diversity in various languages
- Equality between men and women
- Elimination of all forms of prejudice
- World peace and a New world order
- Harmony of religion and science
- Independent investigation of truth
- Principle of Ever-Advancing Civilization
- Universal compulsory education
- Universal auxiliary language

- Obedience to government and non-involvement in partisan politics unless submission to law amounts to a denial of Faith[50]
- Elimination of extremes of wealth and poverty
- Spiritual solutions to economic problems.

---

[50]https://en.wikipedia.org/wiki/Bah

Shrine of the Báb in Haifa, Israel

The Lotus Temple, a Bahá'í House of Worship in New Delhi, India.

Bahá'í House of Worship, Langenhain, Germany

Seat of the Universal House of Justice, governing body of the Bahá'ís, in Haifa, Israel

Jains Religion

Jainism[51] is an ancient religion from India that teaches that the way to liberation and bliss is to live lives of harmlessness and renunciation. The essence of Jainism is concern for the welfare of every being in the universe and for the health of the universe itself.

- Jains believe that animals and plants, as well as human beings, contain living souls. Each of these souls is considered of equal value and should be treated with respect and compassion.

- Jains are strict vegetarians and live in a way that minimises their use of the world's resources.

- Jains believe in reincarnation and seek to attain ultimate liberation - which means escaping the continuous cycle of birth, death and rebirth so that the immortal soul lives forever in a state of bliss.

- Liberation is achieved by eliminating all karma from the soul.

---

[51] http://www.bbc.co.uk/religion/religions/jainism/

- Jainism is a religion of self-help.
- There are no gods or spiritual beings that will help human beings.
- The three guiding principles of Jainism, the 'three jewels', are right belief, right knowledge and right conduct.
- The supreme principle of Jain living is non-violence (ahimsa).
- This is one of the 5 mahavratas (the 5 great vows). The other mahavratas are non-attachment to possessions, not lying, not stealing, and sexual restraint (with celibacy as the ideal).
- Mahavira is regarded as the man who gave Jainism its present-day form.
- The texts containing the teachings of Mahavira are called the Agamas.
- Jains are divided into two major sects; the Digambara (meaning "sky clad") sect and the Svetambara (meaning "white clad") sect.

- Jainism has no priests. Its professional religious people are monks and nuns, who lead strict and ascetic lives.

    Most Jains live in India, and according to the 2001 Census of India there are around 4.2 million living there.

    Fasting is very common in Jain spirituality. Jain fasts may be done as a penance, especially for monks and nuns. Fasting also purifies body and mind, and reminds the practitioner of Mahavira's emphasis on renunciation and asceticism, because Mahavira spent a great deal of time fasting.

    Jainism doesn't have a single founder. The truth has been revealed at different times by a tirthankara, which means a teacher who 'makes a ford' i.e. shows the way. Other religions call such a person a 'prophet'. As great omniscient teachers, Tirthankaras accomplished the highest spiritual goal of existence and then teach others how to achieve it.

Jain nuns meditating

Another temple

Palitana temples[52]

Religious ceremony in India

---

[52]https://en.wikipedia.org/wiki/Jainism#/media/File:Palitana.jpg

Shiniest Religion

The essence of Shinto is the Japanese devotion to invisible spiritual beings and powers called kami, to shrines, and to various rituals. Shinto is not a way of explaining the world. What matters are rituals that enable human beings to communicate with kami. Kami are spirits that are concerned with human beings - they appreciate our interest in them and want us to be happy - and if they are treated properly they will intervene in our lives to bring benefits like health, business success, and good exam results.

Shinto is a very local religion, in which devotees are likely to be concerned with their local shrine rather than the religion as a whole. Many Japanese will have a tiny shrine-altar in their homes. However, it is also an unofficial national religion with shrines that draw visitors from across the country. Because ritual rather than belief is at the heart of Shinto, Japanese people don't usually think of Shinto specifically as a religion - it's simply an aspect of Japanese life. This has enabled Shinto to coexist happily with Buddhism for centuries.

- The name Shinto[53] comes from Chinese characters for *Shen* ('divine being'), and *Tao* ('way') and means 'Way of the Spirits'.

- Shrine visiting and taking part in festivals play a great part in binding local communities together.

- Shrine visiting at New Year is the most popular shared national event in Japan.

- Because Shinto is focussed on the land of Japan it is clearly an ethnic religion.

- Shinto sees human beings as basically good and has no concept of original sin, or of humanity as 'fallen'.

- Everything, including the spiritual, is experienced as part of this world. Shinto has no place for any transcendental other world.

- Shinto has no canonical scriptures.

---

[53] http://www.bbc.co.uk/religion/religions/shinto/ataglance/glance.shtml

- Shinto teaches important ethical principles but has no commandments.
- Shinto has no founder.
- Shinto has no God.
- Shinto does not require adherents to follow it as their only religion.

Entrance to the Grand Shrine of Izumo, one of the main religious centres of Shintō; near …
Kozo Osa/Bon[54]

---

[54]https://www.britannica.com/topic/Shinto/Ritual-practices-and-institutions

Torii (gateway) at the entrance to a Shintō shrine on Mount Hakone, east-central Honshu

Shintoism in Japan

Tao Religion

Taoism is an ancient tradition of philosophy and religious belief that is deeply rooted in Chinese customs and worldview. Taoism is also referred to as Daoism, which is a more accurate way of representing in English the sound of the Chinese word. Taoism is about the Tao. This is usually translated as *the Way*. But it's hard to say exactly what this means. The Tao is the ultimate creative principle of the universe. All things are unified and connected in the Tao.

- Taoism[55] originated in China 2000 years ago
- It is a religion of unity and opposites; Yin and Yang. The principle of Yin Yang sees the world as filled with complementary forces - action and non-action, light and dark, hot and cold, and so on
- The Tao is not God and is not worshipped. Taoism includes many deities, that are worshipped in Taoist

---

[55]http://www.bbc.co.uk/religion/religions/taoism/ataglance/glance.shtml

temples, they are part of the universe and depend, like everything, on the Tao

- Taoism promotes:
    - achieving harmony or union with nature
    - the pursuit of spiritual immortality
    - being 'virtuous' (but not ostentatiously so)
    - self-development
- Taoist practices include:
    - meditation
    - fengshui
    - fortune telling
    - reading and chanting of scriptures

Before the Communist revolution fifty years ago, Taoism was one of the strongest religions in China. After a campaign to destroy non-Communist religion, however, the numbers significantly reduced, and it has become difficult to assess the statistical popularity of Taoism in the world.

Lao Tzu (Laozi) is traditionally described as the founder of Taoism, but modern writers think he is a legendary figure, and that the book attributed to him - the Tao Te Ching - is actually a collection of writings by many different wise people. In that way it's like the Biblical Book of Proverbs. The term Lao Tzu may not be the name of a person, but a reference to 'the old master', meaning the accumulated wisdom of the elders, the wise old men and women of the culture in which Taoism originated. However, at the time the Tao Te Ching was written down there may have been sound political reasons to give it the prestige of being a philosophical treatise by a master philosopher, one who could give lessons to Confucius (as he appears to do at points in the text.). Over the centuries the legend of Lao Tzu developed. The first biography appeared around the 1st century BCE. Later mythological developments cast Lao Tzu in three roles - the original pure manifestation of the Tao as a God, the human philosopher who wrote the Tao Te Ching, and the Buddha.

To suggest that Lao Tzu had no historical existence doesn't disparage him, or Taoism, in any way. Myths have great power and value, and things can be true without having ever actually happened.

At the heart of Taoist ritual is the concept of bringing order and harmony to many layers of the cosmos: the cosmos as a whole (the world of nature), the world or human society, and the inner world of human individuals. Taoist rituals involve purification, meditation and offerings to deities. The details of Taoist rituals are often highly complex and technical and therefore left to the priests, with the congregation playing little part. The rituals involve the priest (and assistants) in chanting and playing instruments (particularly wind and percussion), and also dancing.

One major Taoist ritual is the *chiao* (*jiao*), a rite of cosmic renewal, which is itself made up of several rituals.

A shortened version of the *chiao* is a ritual in which each household in a village brings an offering for the local deities. In the ceremony a Taoist priest dedicates the offerings in the names of the families, performs a ritual to restore order to the universe, and asks the gods to bring peace and prosperity to the village.

As with many ancient religious traditions, an exact date is impossible to determine. Taoist ideas and early writings long precede any organizational structure. The date given here (c. 550 b.c.e.) is generally the time period when a variety of spiritual thinkers were putting their ideas into writing. These writings were not collected as a composite teaching of the "Tao" until the 4th or 3rd century B.C.E.

While Taoists recognize a vast pantheon of gods and goddesses, they do not acknowledge any that are omnipotent or eternal. All the gods, including Laozi, are divine emanations of celestial energy.

Taoism has no centralized authority and different sects have different headquarters. However, the White

Cloud Temple in Beijing is a key center for training for priests and for administration[56].

Intense stick burning at the Taoist temple.

---

[56]http://www.patheos.com/Library/Taoism

Taoist ritual ceremonies

A religious ceremony in Taoism.

Taoist rite at the *Qingyanggong* (Green Goat Temple) in Chengdu

An ancestor worship ceremony led by Taoists at the pyramidal Great Temple of Lord Zhang Hui

Zoroastrianism Religion

Zoroastrianism[57] is one of the world's oldest monotheistic religions. It was founded by the Prophet Zoroaster (or Zarathustra) in ancient Iran approximately 3500 years ago. For 1000 years Zoroastrianism was one of the most powerful religions in the world. It was the official religion of Persia (Iran) from 600 BCE to 650 CE. It is now one of the world's smallest religions. In 2006 the New York Times reported that there were probably less than 190,000 followers worldwide at that time.

- Zoroastrians believe there is one God called Ahura Mazda (Wise Lord) and He created the world.

- Zoroastrians are not fire-worshippers, as some Westerners wrongly believe. Zoroastrians believe that the elements are pure and that fire represents God's light or wisdom.

---

[57] http://www.bbc.co.uk/religion/religions/zoroastrian/history/parsis.shtml

- Ahura Mazda revealed the truth through the Prophet, Zoroaster.
- Zoroastrians traditionally pray several times a day.
- Zoroastrians worship communally in a Fire Temple or *Agiary*.
- The Zoroastrian book of Holy Scriptures is called The Avesta.
- The Avesta can be roughly split into two main sections:
    - The Avesta is the oldest and core part of the scriptures, which contains the Gathas. The Gathas are seventeen hymns thought to be composed by Zoroaster himself.
    - The Younger Avesta - commentaries to the older Avestan written in later years. It also contains myths, stories and details of ritual observances.
- Zoroastrians are roughly split into two groups:
    - The Iranians

> The Parsis

Zoroastrians are not fire-worshippers, as some Westerners wrongly believe. Zoroastrians believe that the elements are pure and that fire represents **God**'s light or wisdom. Zoroaster placed less emphasis on ritual worship, instead focusing on the central ethics of 'Good Words, Good Thoughts and Good Deeds'. Zoroastrian worship is not prescriptive. Its followers can choose whether they wish to pray and how.

Communal worship is usually centred on seasonal festivals (of which the Zoroastrians have many), but there are other opportunities for worshipers to gather, such as the Navjote, the initiation ceremony where a child is accepted into the Zoroastrian fellowship.

Zoroastrians traditionally pray several times a day. Some wear a kusti, which is a cord knotted three times, to remind them of the maxim, 'Good Words, Good Thoughts, Good Deeds'. They wrap the kusti around the outside of a sudreh, a long, clean, white cotton shirt. They may engage in a purification ritual, such as the washing of the hands, then untie and then retie it while reciting prayers.

Prayers are primarily invocational, calling upon and celebrating Ahura Mazda and his good essence that runs through all things. Prayers are said facing the sun, fire or other source of light representing Ahura Mazda's divine light and energy. Purification is strongly emphasised in Zoroastrian rituals. Zoroastrians focus on keeping their minds, bodies and environments pure in the quest to defeat **evil** (AngraMainyu). Fire is seen as the supreme symbol of purity, and sacred fires are maintained in Fire Temples (*Agiaries*). These fires represent the light of God (Ahura Mazda) as well as the illuminated mind, and are never extinguished. No Zoroastrian ritual or ceremony is performed without the presence of a sacred fire.

According to the historical documents[58] and the surveys of writers, any of the Zarathustra's principles

---

[58] http://realhistoryww.com/world_history/ancient/Misc/Elam/Zoroastrian_rel.htm

are confirmed by contemporary ethics, while the other religions have not dealt with them. As an example:

1. Equality between men and women are frequently mentioned in Gatha and we know that in the Persian history, women such as "Pourandokht," has been reigning in Persia. It is interesting that in 1944, following a long discussion, the United Nations in its latest session at Ghahereh, finally came to the conclusion that the only solution of birth control. is the equality of men and women.
2. Cleanliness of water, land, air, and fire is one of the chief characteristics of zoroastrianism and particularly, Herodotus has alluded to the cleanliness of running water in section 138 of his first book in the ancient Persia.
3. There is no mention of the inhumane theory and practice of slavery in zoroastrianism.
4. Another praiseworthy doctrine of Zoroastrians, which is frequently mentioned in Gatha, is

denunciation of laziness. Laziness and taking advantage of the products of others toils is strongly reproached as the act of oppression. Everybody should take it upon himself/herself to relieve the oppressed people from exploitation by others. Everybody should subsist by the fruits of his/her own labor.

5. Idolatry, litholatry, and human made places of worship are reproached in zoroastrianism. "God's house," cannot be made by human beings with mud and stone, it is the soul and heart of them.

6. In Zoroastrianism not only oppression toward human beings is strongly condemned; Gatha frequently reproaches cruelty against animals. Sacrifice of animals by human beings is considered the criminality of mankind against animals.

Important believes of Zoroastrianism

The fire temple for Zoroastrians of Iran in the city Yazd

The wedding ceremony.

A religious ceremony.

Non Religions

Despite the apparent rise in people with no religion, the overall percentage of non-believers is expected to decline[59] as a share of the world's population, according to a new survey from the Pew Research Center.

By 2050, the number of people who identify as atheist, agnostic, or who say they have no particular religion will grow by 100 million, for a total of 1.2 billion people. But the percentage of believers will vastly outpace that growth, expanding by more than 2 billion over the same span of time. As a result, the percentage of non-believers, while growing in real terms, will decrease from 16 to 13 percent of the world's population by 2050.

The study, which classifies non-believers as religions "nones" points out that nones tend to be older, meaning they will die sooner, and have fewer children

---

[59] http://bigthink.com/ideafeed/non-religious-world-population-is-on-the-decline

than people who are associated with religion. In addition, the 10 countries with the largest unaffiliated populations in the world as of 2010 are all expected to decline as a share of the world's population by 2050.

While some have speculated that religious faith decreases as societies become more affluent, there is scant evidence for this trend beyond nations in Western Europe. No such phenomenon occurs in Muslim-majority countries, and in Hindu-majority India, "religious affiliation is still nearly universal despite rapid economic and social change."

China also represents an interesting case study since it does not keep reliable data on religious affiliation, though many believe Christianity is on the rise in the communist country. If that does prove true, the ratio of "nones" could decrease even more by 2050. For those who have lost their religion or never had one, finding a label can feel important. It can be part of a healing process or, alternately, a way of declaring resistance to a dominant and oppressive paradigm.

Finding the right combination of words can be a

challenge though. For a label to fit it needs to resonate personally and also communicate what you want to say to the world. Words have definitions, connotations and history, and how people respond to your label will be affected by all three. If, one way or another, you've left religion behind, and if you've been unsure what to call yourself, you might try on one of these[60]:

Atheist.

The term atheist can be defined literally as lacking a humanoid god concept, but historically it means one of two things. Positive atheism asserts that a personal supreme being does not exist. Negative atheism simply asserts a lack of belief in such a deity. It is possible be a positive atheist about the Christian God, for example, while maintaining a stance of negative atheism or even uncertainty on the question of a more abstract deity like a "prime mover." In the United States, it is important to know that atheist may be the most reviled label for a godless person. Devout

---

[60]http://www.alternet.org/story/155685/no_religion_7_types_of_non-believers

believers use it as a slur and many assume an atheist has no moral core. Until recently calling oneself an atheist was an act of defiance. That appears to be changing. With the rise of the "New Atheists" and the recent atheist visibility movement, the term is losing its edge.

Anti-theist.

When atheist consistently evoked images of Madeline Murray O'Hare, hostility toward religion was assumed. Now that it may evoke a white-haired grandmother at the Unitarian church or the gay kid on Glee, some people want a term that more clearly conveys their opposition to the whole religious enterprise. The term anti-theist says, "I think religion is harmful." It also implies some form of activism that goes beyond merely advocating church-state separation or science education. Anti-theism challenges the legitimacy of faith as a moral authority or way of knowing. Anti-theists often work to expose harms caused in the name of God like stonings, gay bating, religious child maltreatment, genital mutilation, unwanted childbearing or black-collar crime. The New Atheist writers including Christopher Hitchens and Richard Dawkins might better be described as anti-theists.

Agnostic.

Some atheists think of agnostic as a weenie term, because it gets used by people who lack a god-concept but don't want to offend family members or colleagues. Agnostic doesn't convey the same sense of confrontation or defiance that atheist can, and so it gets used as a bridge. But in reality, the term agnostic represents a range of intellectual positions that have important substance in their own right and can be independent of atheism. Strong agnosticism views God's existence as unknowable, permanently and to all people. Weak agnosticism can mean simply "I don't know if there is a God," or "We collectively don't know if there is a God but we might find out in the future." Alternately, the term agnosticism can be used to describe an approach to knowledge, somewhat like skepticism (which comes next in this list).

Skeptic.

Traditionally, skeptic has been used to describe a person who doubts received religious dogmas. However, while agnostic focuses on God questions in particular, the term skeptic expresses a broader life approach. Someone who calls him- or herself a skeptic has put critical thinking at the heart of the matter. Well known skeptics, like Michael Shermer, Penn and Teller, or James Randi devote a majority of their effort to debunking pseudoscience, alternative medicine, astrology and so forth. They broadly challenge the human tendency to believe things on insufficient evidence. Australian comic Tim Minchen is an outspoken atheist who earns a living in part by poking fun at religion. But his most beloved and hilarious beat poem, Storm, smacks down homeopathy and hippy woo.

Freethinker.

Free-thinker is a term that dates to the end of the 17th Century, when it was first used in England to describe those who opposed the Church and literal belief in the Bible. Freethought is an intellectual stance that says that opinions should be based on logic and evidence rather than authorities and traditions. Well known philosophers including John Locke and Voltaire were called freethinkers in their own time, and a magazine, The Freethinker, has been published in Britain continuously from 1881 to the present. The term has gotten popular recently in part because it is affirmative. Unlike atheism, which defines itself in contrast to religion, freethought identifies with a proactive process for deciding what is real and important.

Humanist.

While terms like atheist or anti-theist focus on a lack of god-belief and agnostic, skeptic and freethinker all focus on ways of knowing—humanist centers in on a set of ethical values. Humanism seeks to promote broad wellbeing by advancing compassion, equality, self-determination, and other values that allow individuals to flourish and to live in community with each other. These values drive not from revelation, but from human experience. As can be seen in two manifestos published in 1933 and 1973 respectively, humanist leaders don't shy away from concepts like joy and inner peace that have spiritual connotations. In fact, some think that religion itself should be reclaimed by those who have moved beyond supernaturalism but recognize the benefits of spiritual community and ritual. Harvard Chaplain Greg Epstein dreams of incubating a thriving network of secular congregations.

Pantheist.

As self-described humanists seek to reclaim the ethical and communitarian aspects of religion, pantheists center in on the spiritual heart of faith--the experience of humility, wonder, and transcendence. They see human beings as one small part of a vast natural order, with the Cosmos itself made conscious in us. Pantheists reject the idea of a person-god, but believe that the holy is made manifest in all that exists. Consequently, they often have a strong commitment to protecting the sacred web of life in which and from which we have our existence. The writings of Carl

Sagan reflect this sentiment and often are quoted by pantheists, for example in a "Symphony of Science" video series which mixes evocative natural world images, atonal music, and the voices of leading scientists, and has received 30 million views.

Is it God, Allah or other Deities watching over us?

I have had the experience beyond this life. When I was 72 years, I had a severe Stroke. I was unconscious for 4 weeks and the doctors told my family to prepare for the worst. My sprit seemed to have left my body in an un-conscious way. The doctors put me in a coma, and my spirit was waiting, will I return? I was hoping that the time is not yet to die, I wanted to see my family again.

When I woke up after 4 weeks in a coma, I saw my wife holding my hand, and it was reassuring. I could only say "**Hi**" but, it was **my communication!** I was alive and I wanted to be well again. I could not easily move, but life was returning to me! I was determined at that time to get well again. When I saw the doctor, I could only say 20 words and my right side was paralyzed. But my will-power was there to get better. I then began praying to **God** to regain my strength and learn to walk again. For hours I was moving my toe on my right foot. I was attending all the physiotherapy sessions in the hospital and movement was coming back, slowly, but surely. After spending 5 months in hospital, I was starting to recover. When I was discharged, I walked out of the hospital with a cane and left the wheel chair behind. I was working on my speech which improved to 300 words.

I had the Stroke 6 years ago. I did recover my vocabulary in English (80%) and Hungarian (50%), and my ability to walk is about 90%. I am 100% back at work, working on a publication of an article for a journal (I am a research scientist), and in the evening, I am writing my books (6th one and continuing).

After this review at age 78 years old, I believe that there is a supreme being called God, Allah or other Deities. The gender is neutral but he/she/it watches over us. It is wrong to fight over the love of God. The Supreme Being loves all of us. Through religion, we get together in a congregation and we rejoice in loving one another.

Finally, I wish to dedicate this book to the people who influenced my life significantly, Mr. Nehru and Mr. Gandhi. I met Mr. Nehru in 1958 in Edinburgh and we discussed the Hungarian Revolution. I have visited India 14 times and I have been to the place where Mr. Gandhi was killed.

The quotes from these world leaders have guided me:

"All of us with one voice call one God differently as Parmatma, Ishwara, Shiva, Vishnu, Rama, Allah, Khuda, Dada-Hormuzda, Jehova, God and an infinite variety of names".

"When I admire the wonders of a sunset or the beauty of the moon, my soul expands in the worship of the creator".

"One's own religion is after all a matter between oneself and one's Maker and no one else's" Mahatma Gandhi

"Time is not measured by the years that pass by, instead by the things you do, feel or accomplish"

"Life is like a game of cards. The hand you are dealt is determinism; the way you play it is free will."

Jawaharlel Nehru

www.ingramcontent.com/pod-product-compliance
Lightning Source LLC
Chambersburg PA
CBHW051924160426
43198CB00012B/2032